Why

The book o   ᵤay

Gary Benfold

DayOne

© Day One Publications 1998
First printed 1998

Scripture quotations are from The New King James Version.
© 1982 Thomas Nelson Inc.

British Library Cataloguing in Publication Data available
ISBN 0 902548 76 X

Published by Day One Publications
3 Epsom Business Park, Kiln Lane, Epsom, Surrey KT17 1JF.
☎ 01372 728 300 **FAX** 01372 722 400
e-mail address: ldos.dayone@ukonline.co.uk

Designed by Steve Devane and printed by Clifford Frost Ltd, Wimbledon SW19 2SE

Dedication

To Doctor Rosemary Wool
To you, under God, we owe our sanity
and probably so much more

Job was a godly man who could not understand why he had to suffer so much. His friends could not come up with any satisfying answers. Not even God answered his questions. And yet it was in listening to God that he was freed from turmoil and found peace of heart.

Gary Benfold encourages us to read the book of Job for ourselves, but he does not lead us to ponder every word and turn of phrase in it. Instead, he skilfully guides us through the book's main movement and themes, constantly underlining how it speaks to us today. Brilliant summaries, teaching from elsewhere in scripture, concrete examples, varied and lively illustrations, all combine to drive the lessons home.

Mr Benfold writes simply, but his book is profound. We sense that he understands how we think and knows about our suffering and unhappiness. We therefore listen as he sensitively applies the book of Job to our deepest problems and questions, to the modern issues we face and to the errors that threaten to deceive us.

The book he has written is thoroughly biblical, theologically rigorous and filled with practical help. It points us to Christ, glories in his cross, and convinces us that it is always safe to trust the living God who, in his wisdom, often chooses not to explain himself. It is just the sort of book that so many of us need.

Stuart Olyott

Why Lord? Contents

Although the Lord Jesus said that we need every word of God to live (Matthew 4:4), many people read the Bible as if it is only good in parts! There are whole books of the Bible which the average reader either never reads or barely understands. The Book of Job, although one of the bigger books of the Old Testament with forty-two chapters, is one of those books.

This should not be. Job deals with one of the most common questions of faith and one of the most enduring experiences of humanity: suffering. Why do people suffer? In particular, why do the righteous suffer? Could it be that God does not care? Or is he powerless to act? These questions are often asked as if the Bible says nothing at all about them, but it does. That is what the book of Job is about.

This book is not a commentary on Job. Commentaries deal with every word of the text and confine themselves closely to the Bible book they are examining. What I have tried to do here is to draw out some of the major themes of the book of Job, and to explore their relevance for us today. If this helps us to understand Job and especially if it persuades more people to read Job for themselves, its production will have been worthwhile.

Gary Benfold, February 1998.

The Reign of God

Please read Job chapters 1-2

One Wednesday in March 1996 a gunman burst into a school gymnasium in Dunblane, Scotland, and killed more than a dozen children aged between 4 and 6, a teacher, and finally himself.

A few years ago my wife was visiting a lady in Stoke Mandeville Hospital near our home in Buckinghamshire and heard of a man who had been involved in a car accident nearly two years earlier. He had been paralysed from the waist down and spent almost two years in the hospital. When he was finally allowed home, he was involved in another car accident within twenty-four hours, and re-admitted. This time he had been paralysed from the shoulders down.

Christians are not exempt from apparently senseless suffering. The story of Joni Eareckson is well-known: as a young girl of 17 out for a day's swimming, she dived into too shallow a pool and broke her neck; she has been in a wheel-chair ever since. Less well known is the story of Glenn Chambers, a young man from New York. He had a life-long dream to serve God in Ecuador; at last the day of his departure came. Trying to find some paper to write a quick note to his mother from the airport, he found a sheet with the word 'Why?' printed in large letters in the middle. He scribbled the note, posted it—and that night his aeroplane crashed into a Colombian mountain. When his mother received that last note, the obvious question shouted up at her from the page: 'Why?'

'If there is a God of love, why is there so much suffering in the world?'

Perhaps no question is asked more often than that when Christians try to witness for Christ. We tell others about the magnificent love of God, but they have a problem. What they see of the world does not seem to square with the idea that God is love!

It is **a very real question.** No-one in these television-dominated days can fail to realise that the world is full of suffering. It may be bombs in Bosnia or famine in Africa, but night after night the news is much the same. Suffering, suffering and more suffering.

It is also **a very relevant question.** Suffering is not simply an abstract, faraway thing. It does not just happen 'out there' or to 'someone else.' Some suffer more than others, certainly; but is it not true that all of us suffer in this life? There are no exceptions; if we live long enough, we will all know suffering and grief to a greater or lesser extent.

It is also **a very reasonable question.** When we are on the receiving end, it is only human to ask this question in many forms. 'Why me?' we may ask. 'Am I suffering because I am a sinner? Am I more of a sinner than those who do not suffer so much? Why does God allow me to suffer so much—is it because he does not care about me? Or, if he cares, is he powerless to help?'

Questions like this often erupt from within us at a time when it is hard for us to think rationally. They go round and round in our heads, and only serve to make everything so much worse.

Such questions cannot be answered by looking inside ourselves; it is just here that the book of Job is so helpful. As we examine its teaching, we will see that asking questions is not a sin in itself—although our attitude at the time might be. We will also see (and this is a main lesson of the book of Job) that suffering is not always a sign of sin in our life.

Job is a book about a man who suffered. He was a godly man, but that did not stop a depth of suffering that, happily, most of us are strangers to. In his agony Job asked the very questions we ask, and the book of Job points us in the way of some answers. It by no means tells us everything! But if we want to understand suffering, we can do no better than study Job.

The Drama begins

In the very first chapter of the book we are told something that Job never finds out. We are told that his sufferings stem from a confrontation in heaven.

In the first scene of the book all God's angels appear before him, and Satan is with them. God draws Satan's attention to Job, a godly man.

But Satan responds in a challenging way; Job is only godly, says Satan, because godliness pays. God rewards Job's godliness, and Job is interested in the rewards, not in God. (See 1:9-11.)

But God knows that is not true. To prove his case, God gives Satan permission to take away all Job's property, 'only do not lay a hand on his person' (1:12). So Satan leaves God's presence, and Job loses everything. A black day dawns when one messenger after another brings Job bad news. First his oxen and donkeys are stolen, and his servants killed. Then he hears that his sheep and their shepherds have been killed, and next it is the turn of the camels and their keepers. Finally, worst of all, comes the news that a great wind has destroyed the house with all Job's sons and daughters inside. Every one of them is dead. Although Job must have been crushed by all this news his reaction is the very picture of godly trust. He says, 'Naked I came from my mother's womb, and naked shall I return there. The Lord gave and the Lord has taken away; blessed be the name of the Lord,' (1:21). We are specifically told that no taint of sin marred his reaction (verse 22).

God's case therefore—that Job is godly for its own sake—seems to be proved, and God says so the next time Satan appears before him (2:3). But Satan is ready with his answer. 'Of course Job still worships you,' he says. 'You're still rewarding him! Doesn't he have his health? Isn't that more important than anything else? Take away his health and you'll see how Job **really** feels about you!' (See 2:4,5)

Yet again, God knows his man, and Satan is allowed to steal Job's health. Again there are limits set by God: Job must not die. Once more Satan leaves God's presence, and Job's affliction begins. He becomes ill, and is covered from head to foot with painful sores. We do not know the exact nature of Job's illness, but we know enough! It was an illness that afflicted his whole body, and brought him into the most disgusting condition. When, finally, his friends come to visit him, they are speechless at what they see (2:13)!

There is an important lesson here. We may sing very easily, 'Our God reigns'—and of course it is true, as we shall see. But to sing that in light, and ease, and comfort is one thing. The real test comes when we are in darkness, and illness, and great discomfort. How do we feel then? What do we sing then? Job is a lesson to us, for still his reaction is free of sin. 'Shall we indeed accept good from God, and not accept adversity?' he asks (2:10).

That is the story of the first two chapters in outline; now we need to take a closer look at the main characters in the drama.

The Characters

1. Job

There are many things we are not told about Job—things that perhaps we would like to know. We are not told, for example, **when** he lived; there is some doubt too about **where** he lived. (That is, we are not completely certain where the land of Uz (1:1) actually was.) But the Bible was not written to satisfy our curiosity and these things are really not important. But there are at least two very important things we **are** told about Job.

Firstly **Job was a worshipping man.** The very first verse of the book tells us that he was blameless and upright. Of course, no man is perfect and Job was no exception. But if you had known him you would have been completely unable to fault his life. He was **blameless:** he was not deliberately disobedient to God's perfect law. He was **upright:** he had a standard, a rule for living, and he lived by it. Just as a wall's uprightness can be demonstrated with a plumb-line, so Job's uprightness could be demonstrated by God's law. He was a man who shunned evil. If we are to understand the book of Job at all, it is vitally important to recognise that Job was a righteous man. For this reason, we will return to the subject of Job's innocence later.

For now, let us ask why Job lived such a life. The answer we are given is that Job 'feared God and [therefore] shunned evil.' (1:1).

This **does not** mean that Job lived a trembling, frightened sort of life, terrified that he might make God angry. That is not what 'the fear of the Lord' means in the Bible. It **does** mean that the reality of God's existence dominated Job's life. He knew that one day he would have to face God. One day he would have to 'give account of himself to God' (Romans 14:12)—that is, of the way he had lived and the things he had done.

This made him very careful. Job was a wise man, because 'the fear of the Lord is the beginning of wisdom' (Proverbs 9:10).

One example of Job's godly carefulness is given in verse 5 of chapter 1. Job offered sacrifices **in case** his children had sinned. Today, many people (even some Christians) have a very poor understanding of what sin is and can even talk about 'not sinning.' But Job knew very well that God's standards are high, and it is possible to sin unknowingly or inadvertently. It is not only sin when we deliberately and rebelliously choose to do what God has forbidden. Because our natures are corrupt, and because our understanding of God is imperfect, we may sin without knowing it. But it is still sin, and Job was careful to see that such sins were atoned for.

Secondly, **Job was a wealthy man.** In fact, he was very rich: 'this man was the greatest of all the people of the East' (1:3) and 'greatest' here means 'richest.'

This may surprise some people. We are not used to the godly being rich, **or** to the rich being godly. We know that great wealth usually comes only through the sort of single-minded effort that leaves very little time to attend to our souls. In fact wealth may bring a self-sufficient arrogance that reminds us of the old joke: 'He was a self-made man who worshipped his creator.'

Wealth has many dangers, and so the Bible warns us against riches many times. We forget too easily that what matters most is not this world and our day-to-day living, but the next world, and the day of the Lord. Riches, however much we have, will not be able to help us then. 'Riches do not profit in the day of wrath' (Proverbs 11:4).

In fact, being rich **can** get in the way of our soul's salvation. The rich fall into many temptations (1 Timothy 6:9) which can lead to all kinds of evil deeds (1 Timothy 6:10). Being rich **can** lead us to deny the Lord (Proverbs 30:8,9). The danger is so great that Jesus warned 'It is easier for a camel to go through the eye of a needle than for a rich man to enter the kingdom of God,' (Mark 10:25). The wise man, therefore, is the one who stores up treasures in heaven, not on earth, (Matthew 6:19).

But although it is hard, it is possible to be both godly and very rich. Job was such a man.

2. God

We have already mentioned the second and greatest character in the drama. He is God. It is not enough, though, just to say 'God.' There are many ideas about God in the world, and so the word means different things to different people. Yet there is only one true God, and Job worshipped him. We are told his name, and some things about him.

First, he is LORD. Very early on in the history of Bible translation, it become usual to represent the name of God, Jehovah, by the word LORD, written in capitals. Whenever our versions of the Old Testament read 'LORD' therefore, it means that the Hebrew original has God's name—Jehovah.

In ancient times, names were not chosen because they were attractive, but to say something about the person. So when God tells us that his name is Jehovah, he is telling us something about himself. The name 'Jehovah' is linked to the verb 'to be', and by using this name God is telling us that he is eternal. He is telling us that he is 'the existing, ever-living, absolute, unchangeable One.' [1] He had no beginning; he can never have an end. 'In the beginning (that is, at the beginning of time) God created...' (Genesis 1:1). When time itself began, God already existed. 'From everlasting to everlasting, you are God,' (Psalm 90:2).

Naturally, we find this very difficult to understand; it is completely outside our experience. Everything we know had a beginning. The computer I type at and the page you read both had a beginning. The materials they were made from had beginnings in their turn. We had a beginning, too. There was a time when we did not exist. (I remember trying to explain that to my daughter when she was very young: 'But where **was** I Daddy?' It is not an easy concept; as we grow, we learn to accept it, rather than to understand it.) But God is different. He alone had no beginning. He alone is eternal.

The second thing we are told about God is that he is Lord of the angels. In these chapters, we see God's angels presenting themselves to him. They are under his control; he is their creator and their commander. That is why some translations of the Bible call him 'Lord of hosts', translating 'Jehovah Sabaoth.' 'The 'hosts' are all the heavenly powers, ready to do the LORD's command.' [2] Sometimes,

God uses these angels as messengers (which is what the word 'angel' means). For example God sent the angel Gabriel to Mary the mother of Jesus, and there are many other similar accounts in the Bible. The angels do God's bidding and so they symbolise his power and authority.

The third thing we are told is that God is Lord of space and time. These chapters clearly show us that God is everywhere, and knows everything. Look for example at chapter 2. Satan is asked where he has been, and we are told 'From going to and fro on the earth, and from walking back and forth on it' (2:2). Although Satan is a spiritual creature, and can do many things that are outside mortal men's powers, yet he is limited. He cannot be everywhere at once; if he wants to know what is going on in the earth, he has to roam about to collect his information. But God is different. He knows everything and **is** everywhere precisely because he is God. All creatures are limited by space and time, but God the Creator is not. When he says 'Have you considered my servant Job?' (2:3) God obviously knows all about Job. But he knows all about him without having 'left' heaven. God is everywhere at once.

This is important for this reason. We see in these chapters a great deal about the power of Satan. We see him affecting Job's health, causing the death of Job's family and so on. Sometimes, when Satan's power has been demonstrated from the Bible, people have got the idea that he is as powerful as God—in fact, that there are two Gods in the universe, one good and one bad. This is called **dualism**. But even though Satan is called 'the god of this age' (2 Corinthians 4:4), it is important to realise that he is not God; he is a creature. There is an enormous gulf between God and Satan, more than just a difference of character. In fact, the difference between God and Satan is much, much greater than the difference between Satan and man. Satan and man are created, creatures of time; God is Creator, Lord of eternity.

3. Satan
Satan is our third character; we have met him already. He is an angel; when the angels present themselves before God, he comes too (1:6, 2:1). He is not a good angel; his name means 'adversary' or 'enemy' and that is how we see him in these opening chapters. He is an enemy.

First, he is **the enemy of Job** (and of all mankind). When God commends Job to Satan, singling him out as a real example of godliness, Satan accuses Job of not being godly at all. 'You talk about Job,' says Satan in effect, 'but he's only godly because it pays. You protect him, you bless him—of course he worships you. But if you take away everything he has, you'll see what he is really like' (1:9-11). And he repeats the charge after Job survives the first test, in 2:4-5.

Second, he is **the enemy of God.** The brazen rudeness of the devil in these chapters when he speaks to Almighty God is quite astonishing! Read 1:9-11 and 2:4-5 aloud and you will be able to hear the sneer and hatred in Satan's words. Satan is not like the other angels who present themselves before God. He is the enemy of God, and in one sense the book of Job is about the hatred Satan feels for God.

What we are not told in these chapters is how Satan came to be like this. The Bible does tell us, and we will look at what it says in another chapter. But first, we must look at our three major characters and ask: who is in control?

Who is in control?

We have seen that these first two chapters outline a number of great and traumatic experiences in Job's life. He loses his wealth, his sons and daughters, his health, his reputation and later he comes close to losing his faith too. We all know something of suffering in our experience (because it is true that 'man is born to trouble as the sparks fly upwards'—Job 5:7) but happily most of us do not suffer as much as Job did. But we may still ask—**what** is behind it all? **Why** do people suffer? Is there an order behind everything, or is it just 'the slings and arrows of outrageous fortune'? **Who** is in control?

Clearly, it is not Job!

Throughout the book, Job is bewildered by what is happening all around him. He curses the day of his birth. He cannot understand what is happening, and clearly he has no control over the events that unfold.

Being human, we like to believe the opposite. We make plans for our lives—what we will do, where and what we will study, the work we will do, the heights we will reach—and so on. We take great care to plan the major directions of our lives; and of course this can be a good thing. It becomes a bad thing however when we forget that, ultimately, our destiny is not in our own hands. This kind of self-confidence can be a cause of massive disappointment. As in Job's case, things may happen that come from completely outside and transform every part of our lives. James, the brother of the Lord Jesus, warns us against an arrogant self-confidence: 'Come now, you who say, "Tomorrow we will go to such and such a city, spend a year there, buy and sell, and make a profit"; whereas you do not know what will happen tomorrow. For what is your life? It is even a vapour that appears for a little time and then vanishes away. Instead you ought to say, "If the Lord wills, we shall live and do this or that" (James 4:13-15).

Is it Satan?

If we have read the chapters carefully we will have to admit that Satan is responsible for these tragedies. It is when Satan goes out from the presence of God (1:12, 2:7) that calamities begin to befall Job. In fact we are clearly told that 'Satan... struck Job with painful boils from the sole of his foot to the crown of his head,' (2:7). We can trace the steps by which Satan brought suffering on Job. **First,** he challenges Job's godliness, attempting to provoke God. Without such a challenge, Job would not have suffered. **Next,** he himself afflicts Job. Think about what this means. **Wicked men** are under his control. It is Satan who inspires the Sabeans and Chaldeans to steal oxen and donkeys and camels and kill Job's servants (1:14,15,17). **The weather** is under his control, for lightning destroyed Job's sheep and servants, and a mighty wind killed Job's children (1:18,19). **Disease** is under his control too, for 'Satan... struck Job with painful boils,' (2:7).

The Gospels describe similar events. Wicked men are under his control: when Judas went to betray the Lord Jesus, it was Satan who had entered his heart, (Luke 22:3). When a great storm blew up, threatening to kill Jesus and his disciples (Mark 4:35-41) can we doubt that this was the work of Satan, trying to destroy God's Messiah? And when Jesus heals a crippled woman he describes her as one 'whom

Satan has bound,' (Luke 13:16). The New Testament confirms the Old: Satan has power in the world.

What a powerful creature Satan must be! Our actions, our state of health, our weather—all the circumstances of our lives—may be affected by him. We need to realise the extent of his power, and not treat him lightly. 'The whole world lies under the sway of the wicked one' (1 John 5:19). Because he is powerful, it is dangerous to ignore him. It is dangerous to dabble with the occult, where Satan's power may at times be seen openly. It is dangerous too to play with 'small' sins. That is to underestimate the power of Satan. The chief angel himself is careful of Satan: 'Michael the archangel... dared not bring against him a reviling accusation... but said "The Lord rebuke you." We are not as powerful as Michael; we cannot afford to ignore Satan, or to play with his works!

God is in control!

If we had to stop there it would be a very depressing thing. If **ultimate power** was in the hands of Satan, it would be a terrifying thing—especially for God's people. Satan hates all believers, and he is thoroughly evil. How could we sleep well at night if we were in his unrestrained hands? Thank God, that is not the final truth! These chapters make it clear that **ultimate control** does not belong to Satan; it belongs to God.

Consider first **who takes the initiative.** Yes, Satan challenges Job's godliness. But it was God who brought up Job's name—twice! 'Have you considered my servant Job...?' he asks (1:8 and 2:3). And God knows all things, even the end from the beginning (Isaiah 46:10). That is, he always knows **exactly** how things are going to turn out. Nothing ever takes him by surprise. When God said 'Have you considered my servant Job?' he knew how Satan would respond.

Next, consider **who wields the power.** Certainly, it is Satan who afflicts Job, as we have seen. But we must also see that he **does not** and **cannot** do so until God gives him permission. It is God who allows Satan to say 'Stretch out your hand and touch all that he has,' (1:11,12). It is God who sets the limits: 'only do not lay a hand on his person,' (verse 12). And Satan **does not** exceed the authority that is delegated to him. Later on he challenges those limits: 'Stretch out your hand now and touch his bone and his flesh ...' (2:5) and God gives him permission to do just that. But again, it is God who sets limits which Satan obeys. 'He is in your hand; but spare his life,' says the Lord (2:6). As a result, in spite of all that happens to Job in this book, his life is never in danger. Satan cannot go beyond his authority. The only power Satan has is **delegated** power.

Let me illustrate it this way. I used to be a teacher. Suppose I had said to Tommy, 'Go into the playground and bring Sam Jones to see me.' Now, Tommy could go to Sam Jones, and Sam had to do as Tommy told him. But Tommy's power would not be one of **strength**, it would be one of **authority**; and that authority would have been mine. So it is with Satan and God. When Satan commands lightning to fall, lightning only falls because God has 'loaned' his authority. So, ultimately, it is God and not the devil who is in control.

The rest of Scripture confirms this. All that happens, happens according to the plan of God. God is the one who 'works all things according to the counsel of his will,' (Ephesians 1:11). The Bible allows no exceptions: everything in heaven and earth happens by the will of God. God says 'My counsel shall stand, and I will do all my pleasure,' (Isaiah 46:10), and 'I work and who will reverse it?' (Isaiah 43:13). This is true even of empires and kingdoms; they do not just 'arise' and 'fall' in God's world, for God 'changes the times and the seasons; he removes kings and raises up kings,' (Daniel 2:21). Even sin is under his control. Though God is not a sinner and can never sin, nor be responsible for sin, yet in a way we just cannot understand he rules over sin. Even evil furthers his purposes.

The most evil act ever performed on earth is also the clearest example of this. Wicked men took the Lord Jesus Christ, the holy Son of God, and crucified him. Men sinned when they did this; men were responsible. And yet, they crucified Jesus 'by the determined counsel and foreknowledge of God' (Acts 2:23). If they had not, we could never have been saved. God is in control of everything.

This is a **comfortable** truth. How much better to be in the hands of a good God, a loving heavenly Father, than to be under the power of our cruel and malicious enemy, Satan! It gives meaning to prayer: we can ask God to do things, knowing that he has all power. He is in control.

At the same time it is an **uncomfortable** truth. It causes us many problems. Some of them are theological—for example, how do we explain the origin of evil? Some of them are practical. **Why** does God allow Job (or us) to suffer? If he has the **power** to stop suffering, but does not do so, does it mean that he does not care?

C.H. Spurgeon, the great preacher of the nineteenth century, believed and preached firmly that God is in control. His preaching created a great stir and one man, seeing all the suffering in the world, said 'I do not believe in Mr. Spurgeon's God—if there were such a monster I would not worship him.' We may well understand his point! With all the suffering in the world—with all the suffering of Job before us—if God is in control, how do we avoid concluding that he is a monster?

We must say clearly that God is **good**. Everything he does is **right**. 'Give thanks to the Lord' said a psalmist who knew about suffering in the world 'for **he is good**' (Psalm 106:1).

We must remember that God is **wise**, so much wiser than we are. We do not understand everything he does; some things seem cruel and unnecessary. But that is because we do not know everything! When we do (if we ever do) we will see that in everything God had his own good and wise purposes.

And we must recognise that **faith is not sight**. We believe things now because the Bible tells us they are true—not because we can see their truth for ourselves. Experience and human wisdom are blind guides, and if we follow them we will certainly end up in a ditch! Faith is trust; we trust God when things are dark.

Some years ago my wife Elaine had been ill for a considerable time. She had been so ill in fact that, like Job, we sometimes found our trust in God shaking. Of course, it was hardest for Elaine, and many people tried everything possible to encourage her but we all failed. But God spoke to her himself. Just outside our dining room window we had a forsythia bush, and some time earlier Elaine's father had done some gardening for us. He had pruned the bush—and we thought he had killed it! It was small and bare; surely too small and bare ever to grow again. Yet the following spring it bloomed and blossomed as never before in great cascades of golden yellow. Looking at that bush in its glory one day, Elaine read the words 'My Father is the gardener' (John 15:1, NIV). Those few words helped more than anything else could have done. It helped both of us to trust our heavenly Father. For a long time it seemed to us that **we** had been pruned too severely. But our Father is the gardener. Not everything he does **seems** wise at the time; nevertheless, everything he does **is** both wise and good.

God is in control, and has a wise purpose in everything. We all have to learn to trust him when we cannot see what that purpose may be. We have to learn to wait for those cascades of golden yellow in our lives. God is in control of everything. Faith says 'Hallelujah—the Lord God omnipotent reigns.'

Chapter 1 Notes

1   **T.C. Hammond,** *In Understanding Be Men.* IVP.
2   **G.T. Manley** in *New Bible Dictionary.* IVP.

'More things in heaven and earth...'

Please read Job 1:6 - 2:10

Much of our difficulty in understanding life comes from the simple fact that we can only see the material world. Life for us is made up of working, eating and sleeping. We are involved in human relationships which sometimes give great joy and sometimes great sorrow. We look after (or neglect!) our bodies—taking note of the latest trends in diet, exercise and health-care. We live our lives for their given length, and then we die. Many people make the mistake of living as if that is all there is—a physical life, a material world, human relationships. But there is another dimension to life, the spiritual dimension; though invisible it is very real.

No part of the Bible gives us a clearer picture of the heavenly, spiritual dimension to earthly life than the early chapters of Job. Yet we are so used to the material world that we find these chapters difficult. They raise puzzling questions—for example, the heavenly conferences that we see in the first two chapters. On two occasions we are told that the angels of God came before God, and Satan himself appeared with them. Are we meant to take this literally? Does God summon Satan to stand before him? Does Satan taunt God? Does God respond by giving him permission to cause disasters? Can any or all of human suffering be explained in this way? What of the wars and natural disasters that are always present in the world; are there spiritual, evil forces behind them?

The Bible answers clearly that there are such spiritual forces at work and that we are to take this passage in Job at its face value. This book presents itself as history, and is accepted as history by other parts of Scripture. The Bible regards Job as a real man (Ezekiel 14:14, 20) and his story as a true story (James 5:11). It is important not to bring presuppositions to the Bible and say 'Such a thing does not happen; therefore this bit of the Bible is mythical, or legendary.'

But although we must take this passage at its face value we must also avoid reading into it things that are not there. We may not, for example, read into it the insinuation that God responds to Satan's taunts because God feels threatened by them. We may respond to taunts because we feel threatened and need to prove ourselves; but God is not like us. What we are told here about these heavenly conferences is in complete harmony with the rest of Scripture. And it is this teaching that we have to consider in this chapter.

There is a war on

The Christian life is a struggle. The New Testament letters were written because Christians were finding it difficult to be Christians. Sometimes it was a struggle to keep the faith; all sorts of errors and heresies troubled the early churches. Sometimes it was a struggle just to keep being a Christian in the midst of a godless world. The world was no more sympathetic to Christianity then than it is now; the early Christians were mocked and persecuted for their faith. Persecution was often so great that their lives were in danger. Some, of course, actually lost their lives for their faith: Stephen and James were both martyred (Acts 7 and 12). Peter had to warn his readers about 'fiery trials' (1 Peter 4:12). It was not just a struggle but a battle to be a Christian.

A spiritual battle

When he wrote to the church in Ephesus, Paul wrote about that battle. He was writing to people he knew; he had preached the gospel to them and almost died in a riot that was stirred up deliberately to stop him preaching. Knowing that the members of this church were still undergoing persecution, he wrote to help them. But the way he helps them might, at first sight, seem surprising. He points out that, in reality, the struggle is even greater than they can see. Part of Ephesians chapter 6 reads like this: 'We do not wrestle against flesh and blood, but against principalities, against powers, against the rulers of the darkness of this age, against spiritual hosts of wickedness in the heavenly places. Therefore take up the whole armour of God, that you may be able to withstand in the evil day, and having done all, to stand.'

Paul tells the Christians in Ephesus that their struggle is not simply against flesh and blood; behind those flesh and blood problems are what he calls 'rulers of the darkness of this age [and] spiritual hosts of wickedness in the heavenly places.' He introduces us to a world of spiritual wickedness. He tells us that behind our strugglings and sufferings are spiritual forces of evil.

There is a spiritual battle going on, with the spiritual forces of good against the spiritual forces of evil. Christians do not understand this fully, and it is certainly one of those topics that twentieth century man loves to ridicule. 'How can people in a nuclear age take these things so seriously?' we are asked. Devils and demons and spiritual battles in heavenly places belong to the same realm as fairies and goblins!

The enemy

Nothing is quite so characteristic of twentieth century man as intellectual arrogance. Having made so much progress in knowledge in many areas in this century, modern man is now confident that if he does not know it all then he at least knows most of it! Many view religion itself as outdated; others accept that there may be a God, but certainly not a devil. But today's man needs to be confronted with his ignorance. There are many things we do not know and there are many areas which cannot be scientifically analysed. If we want to know about the spiritual realm, there is only one way we can learn; we must listen to the Holy Spirit. He has spoken in Scripture; and it is from Scripture therefore that we must learn. The reality of the devil, and of spiritual warfare, is taught throughout the Bible.

The devil is a person, not a force. He is a created being; he is not God. He is not equal to God. He was originally created good because God cannot create anything evil. He is one of the 'all things' that were created both **by** and **for** God (Colossians 1:16).

Two particular Biblical passages are traditionally believed to speak of the devil's origin. In the first passage, the prophet Ezekiel refers to the devil's creation and 'fall': 'You were the seal of perfection, full of wisdom and perfect in beauty. You were in Eden, the garden of God; every precious stone was your covering... you were the anointed cherub who covers; I established you; you were on the holy mountain of God; you walked back and forth in the midst of fiery stones. You were perfect in your ways from the day you were created, till iniquity was found in you. By the abundance of your trading you became filled with violence within, and you sinned; therefore I cast you as a profane thing out of the mountain of God; and I destroyed you, O covering cherub, from the midst of the fiery stones. Your heart was lifted up because of your beauty; you corrupted your wisdom for the sake of your splendour; I cast you to the ground...' (28:12-17). In the context, Ezekiel is speaking about the King of Tyre; but as we read it, we become aware that there is more here than the pride and downfall of an earthly King. The prophet is describing the devil and the pride that caused his downfall. Another prophet, Isaiah, says more about this. Isaiah too seems at first to be talking about an earthly king, but again, there is plainly a deeper truth behind his words. 'How you are fallen from heaven, O Lucifer, son of the morning! How you are cut down to the ground, you who weakened the nations! For you have said in your heart: "I will ascend into heaven, I will exalt my throne above the stars of God; I will also sit on the mount of the congregation, on the farthest sides of the north; I will ascend above the heights of the clouds, I will be like the Most High." Yet you shall be brought down to Sheol, to the lowest depths of the Pit' (Isaiah 14:12-15).

If these passages do refer to the devil, they show that he was originally created good, but he rebelled against God and was cast out of heaven for his sin. This is consistent with what the Lord Jesus Christ says in Luke chapter 10. 'I saw Satan fall like lightning from heaven.' Scripture also teaches that when Satan rebelled, others rebelled with him and they were all cast out of heaven. Revelation 12:4 indicates that as many as one third of the celestial created beings went with him. Those beings continue to exist and they continue to hate God, God's word and God's world. They continue to have an influence in God's world, and their only desire is to destroy it, and the work and grace of God.

It is thought by many today to be really rather silly to believe in a personal devil. This is partly because of the way he has been portrayed; a creature with pitchfork, horns and tail—the cartoonists even manage to make him look quite jolly! It is easy not to believe in a devil like that!

But in the Bible the devil is not like that at all. He is a spiritual being of great power; he is called the destroyer, (1 Corinthians 10:10, John 10:10) the deceiver, (Revelation 12:9) a liar and the father of lies, (John 8:44) a murderer, (John 8:44) the prince of the power of the air, (Ephesians 2:2) and the serpent (Genesis 3:1, Revelation 12:9). He is called the god of this age (2 Corinthians 4:4), and likened both to a roaring lion seeking people to devour (1 Peter 5:8) and a thief who comes to steal to kill and to destroy, (John 10:10).

The bible's teaching helps us to understand the state of the world today. The genocides of Hitler and Stalin, mass murders by terrorists, widespread abuse of children and the ever increasing ungodliness of the world are all easier to explain if there is a devil than if there is not. There is a devil; Jesus and the writers of the gospels clearly believed in him, and because of him there is a spiritual battle going on.

The devices of the devil
The apostle Paul says 'we are not ignorant of his devices,' (2 Corinthians 2:11); by studying exactly how Satan attacks Job we will find at least seven devices he uses here.

1: The devil uses slander
'Well yes, God. Job does worship you. You're right, I cannot fault his life. But he doesn't worship you because he cares about you. He worships you because it pays him to do so.' That is what he says about Job (1:9-11 and 2:4-5). He is a slanderer; when we slander others or impugn their motives we are doing the work of the devil. One of the most neglected parts of personal holiness is the control of the tongue! 'See how great a forest a little fire kindles! And the tongue is a fire, a world of iniquity. The tongue is so set among our members that it defiles the whole body, and sets on fire the course of nature; and it is set on fire by hell,' (James 3:5-6).

2: He lies
John 8:44 tells us that the devil is not only a liar by nature, but the father of lies. He was a liar from the beginning and that means, of course, that

he is thoroughly unscrupulous. In this spiritual battle he is not honourable! It is his very nature to be deceitful, to be devious, to be a liar.

3: He uses his considerable power to harm Job

These chapters show something of the variety of personal attacks that are open to Satan. He took away Job's wealth, brought about the death of those close to him and brought great illness on Job himself. Satan has no scruples: this is no 'just war'! He attacks the weak, the very young and the very old—anything and everything he can.

4: He exercises a cruel persistence

When the various servants of Job come in the first chapter to tell him about the disasters that have befallen him, there is almost an echo. They all use the same words: 'and I alone have escaped to tell you.' It becomes a cruel chorus—'to tell you, to tell you, to tell you.' We can easily imagine how that recurring phrase would gradually undermine Job's strength and faith. The simple fact that the same phrase is coming again and again and again adds a 'devilish' dimension to the whole thing. Even before he hears of his children's death, Job's strength has been undermined in that subtle way.

5: He uses family and friends to further his spiritual attack

It was Job's wife who said, 'Do you still hold to your integrity? Curse God and die' (2:9). She should have been a support to him, but Satan used her instead.

When the devil attacked the Lord Jesus Christ, he used Peter. Jesus had just explained that the cross was before him and Peter said 'No, Lord, not so. Never. You cannot go that way.' And Jesus said to him, 'Get behind me Satan' (Matthew 16:23). He knew who it was that was attacking him. He knew who it was that was ultimately in control of Peter's tongue. Peter was very close to the Lord Jesus and so the devil used him to try to undermine Jesus' faith, resolution and strength.

6: He undermines Job's standing with others

That is the point of the appearance of Job's friends at the end of chapter two. There are three 'rounds' of speeches from these friends that take up the bulk of the book. Each one makes three speeches (except Zophar, who only manages two). Some of these are long speeches, and there are different emphases in different speakers and in different rounds. But all that these men say in twenty-eight chapters (that is, chapters 4-31) can be summarised like this: 'Job, you have brought it on yourself. Although you seem to be righteous, there must be some secret sin hidden in your life that has caused all this.' Who told them so? Who slandered Job in the hearts of his friends? Who destroyed his reputation and so undermined Job's standing with others? The devil. It is easy for any of us to pass judgement on others, and so to do the devil's work. And he may actually cause friends who come to 'help' us to set about us like devouring lions. Job's friends are not warm and sympathetic to him in his troubles. They are cold and rigid, out not to help, but to prove that Job has sinned.

7: He uses theology for his own ends.
We will see that there is actually very little wrong with the theology of these three friends. Their mistake was that they applied their theology to Job in inappropriate ways, without any evidence, and refused to consider the possibility that they might be wrong. When Job says to them 'But you are wrong' they do not listen. When he says to them, 'Yes, if I were in your place, I could talk like that,' or defends himself against particular charges, as in 'I made a covenant with my eyes not to look lustfully at a girl,' (31:1, NIV) or 'I delivered the poor who cried out' (29:12) or 'I put on righteousness and it clothed me' (29:14)—they will not believe him. They will not even consider the possibility that they might be wrong. The devil is at work, and these are some of the devices he may use with us.

Remedies
We are in a battle against Satan and his hordes. Is victory possible or are we doomed to a life of constant defeat?

Many well-meaning Christians have a set of favourite slogans that they use to meet any trouble—especially other people's troubles! Some will say, 'Just look to Jesus; he'll sort it out.' Of course there is some truth there; but there is more to the spiritual battle than that. Worse, others say, 'Let go and let God,' which cannot be fitted into the New Testament picture of spiritual battle at all. 'We **wrestle** against principalities and powers,' says Paul. He does not say, 'You're struggling too much. Stop it. Let go and let God.' He says, 'Take up the whole armour of God'. He says, 'Put on this part of the armour and that part so that you may be able to stand in the evil day.' And he writes the New Testament letters with detailed instructions telling us how we are to behave, telling us to curb our tongues, to watch our doctrine, and so on. Why does he not simply say, 'Just look to Jesus and it'll be all right'? Because the Christian life is a battle, and battles are not won by slogans.

Job withstood the devil's first onslaught when he said, 'The Lord gave, and the Lord has taken away. Blessed be the name of the Lord' (1:21). Then he withstood the second onslaught with patience, saying, 'Shall we indeed accept good from God and shall we not accept adversity?' (2:10). Where did he find that strength when his world was collapsing around him? That's a question the Bible answers for us: 'The people who know their God shall be strong,' says Daniel (11:32). 'Those who wait on the Lord shall renew their strength,' says Isaiah (40:31). The strength that prepared him to stand up against such dreadful onslaughts undoubtedly came from the life he had lived **before** the devil was let loose on him. It came from his real, personal communion with God. Job was able to stand because he knew God in a close, experimental way because of the way he had lived his life **before** disaster struck. It was not temperament but training that enabled Job to stand.

If we are to stand firm when difficult days arrive, we too need to prepare. Though it is important to have lives of integrity, on its own it is not enough. Like Job, we must develop our communion with God, to know him and walk with him.

Walking with God

If we are to walk with God there at least three things we must do. The first is, that we must read the word of God, the Bible. 'Your word I have hidden in my heart, that I might not sin against you...' says the psalmist

(Psalm 119:11). It is spiritual food to make us strong; we must be regular readers, not occasional dippers. God has spoken in the Bible, and as we read it we get to know him more closely.

Secondly, we must live prayerful lives—a part of each day must be set aside so that we can talk to our heavenly Father. When Paul talks about the armour of God, and what Christians must do to stand in the evil day, he ends by saying 'praying always with all prayer and supplication in the Spirit,' (Ephesians 6:18). There is no substitute for this; the Bible makes so many promises about prayer, and teaches so many times that Christians should pray, pray continually, and pray perseveringly, that it is nothing short of amazing how little time most Christians give to prayer. But if we are to be spiritually strong, it must be a priority.

Thirdly, we must regularly attend a church where God is truly loved and worshipped. Too many professing Christians nowadays regard church simply as an option when they need it, rather than a family to which they belong. Others are regular attenders at a building called a church, but the message preached there is far from the gospel of Jesus. A true church is the pillar and ground of the truth (1 Timothy 3:15) and Christians are urged 'let us consider one another in order to stir up love and good works, not forsaking the assembling of ourselves together, as is the manner of some, but exhorting one another...' (Hebrews 10:24,25).

In these ways we get to know God; and we must be doing these things in our more easy days, if we are to have strength for the difficult ones. If we want to stand like Job stood, we must live like Job lived.

Someone may argue, though, that of the three things I have mentioned, Job practised only one, that is prayer (1:5). He had no Scriptures, and no church. But that would be a superficial response. Although he had no Scriptures, he was not without revelation from God. In those days, as the last chapters of the book show, God communicated directly; we may be sure that Job used that revelation as carefully as I am urging that we should use the Scriptures. Though there was no 'local church' in the New Testament sense, God still had his people, and fellowship with them was important.

The Christian who bears bright testimony in days of darkness is almost always the one who has laid up spiritual provisions in the good times. Jean is a retired lady who for many years has suffered ill-health of various kinds. Often different kinds of ill-health have plagued her at the same time, so that the doctors have to juggle her medications to avoid them fighting it out! For very long periods of time, she has been unable to attend church; and over the last few years Jean has been so ill that it is a rare privilege to see her at church. Sometimes, her powers of concentration are so weak that she cannot read the Bible; and in her family devotions she struggles to concentrate enough just to be able to say 'Amen' at the end. Yet, throughout, she has known much of the closeness of God and continued to bear testimony to his love and faithfulness. Recently she was well enough at last to go on holiday; and while walking in Scotland she fell and badly broke her shoulder. Once more, she was laid up at home for months! But still Jean trusts God and insists that he knows what he is doing. How is her faith maintained when she is hardly able to hear or read the word of God? For nearly fifty years Jean has been 'squirreling away' her supplies; regular, disciplined times of prayer and Bible reading for nearly half a century are undoubtedly providing nourishment now that she is unable to dig for fresh food. Faith is not an elastic band, that suddenly stretches to meet whatever we may demand of it. It is a muscle that needs to be trained and developed and strengthened through constant exercise, so that, when a time of great need comes, we have strength to respond.

Things may be well with you now. Thank God. Especially if you are young in years or young in the faith you may not have known real trouble; God protects his little ones. But right now, while things are well with you, you need to be laying up strength against the onslaughts of the devil. 'Be sober, be vigilant; because your adversary the devil walks about like a roaring lion, seeking whom he may devour. Resist him, steadfast in the faith,' says Peter (1 Peter 5:8,9). Testing times will come! You need to get to know your God. Many of us are too ready to protest that we do not have time. Tomorrow, next month, next year or maybe even next decade we will have more time. Then tomorrow, next month, next year, next decade comes and we always have less! As we grow older our responsibilities become greater. The demands on our time grow more and more. We always seem to have less time this year than last year. So there will never be a better time: even now we need to be laying up spiritual strength, getting to know our God.

The ultimate remedy

One thing is more important than all, and we need to return to it again and again. 'God demonstrates his own love toward us, in that while we were still sinners, Christ died for us,' (Romans 5:8). We have to learn, in our hearts as well as our heads, that the foundation of faith and the great proof of the love of God is in the cross at Calvary. Times may well come in our lives when the only thing that will hold us is the cross. Everything may seem bleak, with life in a turmoil, just as Job's was. Almost inevitably then the question comes: 'How can God really love me if he allows this to happen to me?' Our circumstances will provide no answer. We will not feel any better by singing, 'Always look on the bright side of life'! But there is an answer. The only way we will know that God loves us is to remember that he sent his Son to die for us. The only anchor we will have is that 'the Son of God loved me and gave himself for me,' (Galatians 2:20). There may well be times when every star in the heavens goes out, but that great star will shine. Learn to dwell often at the cross. Job did not know what we know about the cross, but he did know something, as we will see. He did know that he had a Redeemer. We know more than he did, and it follows therefore that we ought to be able to stand firmer and stronger and longer than he did. Let us dwell often at the cross. We must never move away from it. We must read those passages in the gospels that speak of it, and never let a day go by without thanking God for it. We must spend time there, at Calvary, and meditate on it if we are to stand firm in troubled days.

It is good news to know that we can stand in difficult days; it is even better news to know that Satan is a defeated foe. Let us turn now to that defeat.

The devil's defeat

We have already seen that God is in ultimate control; nothing is able to give us more courage than that! Another great truth of the Scripture to encourage us is the defeat of the devil. There are at least four aspects to this defeat.

1. He is defeated in God's general providence

By 'God's general providence' I mean everything that happens in the world. Every Christian ought to have memorised Romans 8:28: 'And we know that all things work together for good to those who love God.' This means that whenever the devil is at work in our life, or whenever the devil is doing evil things in society, the nations and the world, God is also at work there and will bring everything to the ultimate good of his own people. God in his sovereign providence continually and constantly defeats the schemes of the devil, and triumphs always to his own glory and our good. Whatever the devil does it rebounds ultimately to the glory of God and the good of his children. That is what happened eventually with Job; the good news is that it happens still.

2. He is defeated once and for all at the cross

The life of Jesus was one long triumph against the devil. He triumphed against the devil at his temptation, when the devil tried to turn Jesus aside from the path before him (Luke 4:1-13). He triumphed again in the garden of Gethsemane when tempted to give up and turn away from the cross (Luke 22:39-44). There were many other times too in his life when Jesus was really tempted; Luke tells us that after the temptations the devil left him 'until an opportune time,' (4:13). Yet every time the devil returned, the Lord Jesus triumphed.

But the greatest triumph of the Lord Jesus was on his cross. At Calvary the devil thought he had won at last! Yet what was actually happening was that Christ was defeating him once and for all and making a display of those wicked powers, triumphing over them by the cross, (Colossians 2:15). Jesus broke the bands of death. He robbed, plundered and bound the strong man, (Luke 11:21). The devil is defeated. As Wesley sang, 'The keys of death and hell are to our Jesus given,' (see Revelation 1:18). Jesus Christ has triumphed.

3. He is defeated in the life of every believer

Do you feel defeated? Most of us do some of the time, and some of us do all of the time! And there is certainly a reason for that; we are still sinners, and have certainly sinned this week—even today! So it is very easy to feel defeated again. But we are not defeated: the fact that we long to be better is proof of that. We are showing by our desires that we still belong to Christ. Where will we go when we die? To heaven to be with the Lord Jesus Christ. Whatever the devil may unleash on us, we will triumph, because Jesus has promised: 'I give them eternal life and they shall never perish,' (John 10:28). Remember how Jesus puts that so graphically to Peter: 'Oh Peter, Satan has been asking for you. Satan wants you Peter. He wants to sift you as wheat. But I have prayed for you,' (see Luke 22:31). What a difference that makes! 'But I have prayed for you, that your faith should not fail.' Afterwards, Peter's faith faltered, but it did not fail: in Peter's life, Satan was defeated. The same is true of the life of every true believer. Every sinner who gets to heaven is a defeat for Satan; and every sinner, without exception, who truly trusts Christ gets to heaven.

4. He is defeated at the end of the age

Scripture assures us that the time is coming when the devil and all his followers will be cast into the lake of fire, (See Revelation 20:14,15 and Matthew 25:41). There they will be tormented for ever and ever, even as they have tormented others. The devils themselves know that it is coming; one of the demons that Jesus cast out said: "What do you want with us, Son of God? Have you come here to torture us **before the appointed time?**" (Matthew 8:29, NIV). They knew, and they still know, about the appointed time.

The final victory

Job and his friends could only see what was happening in the material world. He was puzzled by it, **they** thought they knew the reason. Neither Job nor his friends could see the spiritual battle that was going on that **really** explained all that had happened.

We too are part of that battle. Like Job and his friends, we see only what happens to us or our friends without seeing the explanation. Unless we recognise that there really **is** a spiritual battle we will flounder; unless we realise that there is a victory, we will despair!

Victory is sure. At the end of the age there will be a new heaven and a new earth, in which righteousness dwells, (2 Peter 3:13). No evil will ever be allowed there. The walls of hell will be built exceeding high, and the fires of hell will be stoked exceeding hot. This is the final defeat for the devil and his angels, and there will be no escape. He is a defeated foe. 'Hallelujah! The Lord God Omnipotent reigns.'

'Fools Rush In...'

Please read Job 3:1 - 4:21

Asterix the Gaul has a dog called Dogmatix. When I was an undergraduate I discovered theology, and I was so concerned that everybody else should discover it as well that I earned a reputation for being dogmatic. Somebody then gave me a badge that they found in a Weetabix packet which said 'I dig Dogmatix.' As I look back I am sure it was intended as a friendly criticism, but I managed to take it as a compliment. I wore the badge for several days until it fell to pieces. After all, theology is a good thing.

Many years later, I still love theology. I still believe it is a good thing. But I now know that it can bring its problems. Sometimes it is possible for those of us who take an interest in theology to be too much bound by our theological system. We become so sure that what we believe is right, that we cannot see what is in front of our very eyes. As a result we may become overbearing; there is such a thing as a 'trouble with theology' and it is to that we must turn.

The story so far is that Job has suffered. He has suffered the loss of his children as they all die in the same day. He has suffered the loss of the greater portion of his riches. He has suffered (and is still suffering) a very painful and disfiguring skin disease, from the soul of his foot to the crown of his head.

We know some things that Job does not; he does not know about the spiritual warfare behind his suffering. Satan has said that Job's faith is purely mercenary; he serves God (says Satan) because it pays him to do so. But God has denied this: who is right? Can a man endure what Job endures and still love God? Can Job endure all this and still serve God?

Job's friends—Eliphaz, Bildad and Zophar—hear about his suffering. They are concerned for him and they have come to see him. When they see him they discover that he is far worse off than they had realised. They are so confounded, dumbfounded and dumbstruck by his sufferings that they sit in silence for seven days. In the traditional

Eastern way of expressing sorrow they tear their robes, sprinkle dust on their heads and sit on the ground for seven days and seven nights without saying a word. (That is arguably the last wise thing they do in the whole book!) Job sits with them in silence for seven days and then begins to speak to them (Chapter 3). He describes for them the depth of his invisible, internal suffering; he curses the day of his birth and wishes that, if he had to be born at all, he could have died at birth. In chapter four, his friends begin to respond to him. Although I have asked you, for this chapter, to read chapters three and four of Job, we will in fact be looking at material through most of the book and in particular chapters four to thirty one. These chapters are taken up with three rounds of speeches by Job's three friends, Eliphaz, Bildad and Zophar, and Job's response to those speeches. They are very repetitive, so we will not be looking at them in detailed order, but drawing themes from them; that will mean quite a bit of turning to and fro, but I hope that you will find it a helpful way of considering this large passage.

These three men are not good comforters! They are not the sort of people you would want to come and see you if you were having difficulties or were depressed. They are no help to Job at all; he is being quite charitable when he calls them 'miserable comforters' (16:2)! So it may be a surprise to realise that a good deal of what they say is true and confirmed by other Scriptures; very, very often these men have their doctrine right! Let us look at some examples. Chapter four verse 8 says 'Those who plough iniquity and sow trouble reap the same.' Compare that with Galatians 6:7: 'God is not mocked; for whatever a man sows, that he will also reap.' Eliphaz in the same speech (5:17) says, 'Happy is the man whom God corrects; therefore do not despise the chastening of the Almighty.' Compare that with Hebrews 12:5,6 where the writer quotes Proverbs 3:11,12 and says almost exactly the same thing.

Furthermore, Zophar says in chapter 11 'God exacts from you less than your iniquity deserves' (verse 6). In other words, 'Job you are not receiving the full deserts of your sin. If God were to give you everything you deserve, you would be suffering far more than you are suffering now.' We know that he was right; Scripture teaches that all sin deserves eternal hell; Job was a sinner but not in hell, so what Zophar says is undeniably true.

In some senses then these men are wise men, the sort of men Job looks up to (15:10). But yet they are shockingly poor comforters. What went wrong?

Trouble 1: They are unfeeling

First of all they show no sympathy with Job's plight and no understanding of what he is actually feeling. To them, this human tragedy seems to be only an abstract problem in moral theology. It is as if they are sitting an examination with the question: 'How do you explain the suffering of a man like Job?' To answer it, they list certain theological truths that seem to apply, and some deductions that follow from them. Then they feel they have the answer: 'Job must have been a great sinner!' Poor Job is broken-hearted, but for them the problem is merely academic. They do not seem to care, either about his losses or his sickness. They show no sympathy with the way he is feeling, no sympathy with the circumstances. In short, they are simply inhuman.

It is all too easy to be guilty of that. On the morning after the Gulf War broke out an American pilot, coming back from the first bombing mission over Iraq, was asked to describe what he had seen almost as soon as he climbed out of his aeroplane. He compared it to a great fireworks display on July 4th. A little later in the House of Commons one MP verbally attacked this man for having compared the bombing of Baghdad to a fireworks display. However valid his point may have been, that particular member of parliament showed no understanding and no compassion towards that pilot at all. He had just returned successfully from his first ever bombing raid. We can guess at the mixture of emotions that he would be feeling: relief that he had made it back alive; delight in his own skill; shame to be feeling delight at all in such a fatal skill. With all that, there would have been the euphoria that is bound to accompany such an escape from death. Then, without giving him any time for reflection, someone confronted him with a microphone and said, 'Now tell me what it looked like.' It is not surprising if he gave answers that he may have regretted later. Yet he was criticised for it, from the comfort and safety of the British Houses of Parliament, in a most unfair way. It is easy to criticise others without standing where they stand or trying to understand what is going on in their hearts and in their minds at the time. Job's comforters were like that; they had no real sympathy for Job.

Let me give another though quite different example. As a young minister I was once with a group of ministers when they were told that one of their members (absent at the time) had been guilty of very serious sin, very gross sexual immorality. As the story unfolded I stood back watching to see how these godly men would react. It was very moving to see that their first instinctive reaction was sympathy for the fallen sinner. 'How difficult it must have been for him to live with that knowledge for so long. How difficult the circumstances must have been that pushed him into such sin,' and so on. Great concern welled up from within them, and these were the very first things they said. It was only later that they began to talk about the discipline that was necessary and what the Scriptures said about the need to remove that person from ministry. I remember being thrilled by that; there, I was convinced, was the beating heart of Christ, not prepared to condemn (see John 8:1-11). They were full of sympathy and understanding. There was a feeling of 'There but for the grace of God go I.'

Job's comforters felt no true sympathy at all, in spite of their long silence. If any one of them had said 'I can understand how you must be feeling. If I suffered like you, I would probably react very badly,' it would have made all the difference in the world. But no-one did. Their attitude was the exact opposite. 'Oh now come on,' said Eliphaz in effect, 'Your words have upheld him who was stumbling, and you have strengthened the feeble knees, you have been a pastoral counsellor, telling others to put their trust in God. Now a little bit of trouble comes to you and it strikes you with dismay' (4:1-5). He did not feel what Job felt; he did not seem to understand there are limits to human endurance and did not recognise that Job had been pushed to the edge of those limits.

Thank God that God himself is not like that. 'He knows our frame, he remembers that we are dust' (Psalm 103:14). When we sin, we must remember that God knows about the temptations that pushed us there. He knows our circumstances. This does not excuse our sin and must never encourage us to sin; but the Lord Jesus came to save, not condemn. He knows our frame 'from the inside'. He has been tempted in all points as we are. These 'comforters' of Job were hard and cold; they showed no sympathy with his plight.

True holiness is never unfeeling or insensitive. Our Lord Jesus was the holiest man of them all, but he was never uncaring. He hated sin; everything in his holy nature cried out against it. Yet he cared, and still cares, about the sinner. When he looked on the crowds, full of sin as they were, we are not told that he thought 'They deserve all they get.' Instead, we are told 'he was moved with compassion for them, because they were weary and scattered, like sheep having no shepherd,' (Matthew 9:36). A little bit of compassion goes a long way; true Christlikeness will make us very compassionate indeed.

Trouble 2: They are unjust

The second mistake Job's friends made was to accuse him of sin without any evidence of it. It is quite remarkable how little has changed over the centuries. When we are going through something dreadful often the first thing to happen is that some Christian will bound up to us, grinning from ear to ear, and say 'Just trust in the Lord and it will be all right.' Their next reaction is usually to say, 'It is your own fault.' That is what Job's friends do next.

At first, they make general accusations. Eliphaz starts in chapter 4 verse 7: 'Remember now, who ever perished being innocent? Or where were the upright ever cut off? Even as I have seen, those who plough iniquity and sow trouble reap the same...' In simple terms he says, 'If you are experiencing trouble Job it is because you deserve it.'

Job is quite prepared to agree that all men are sinners. He says as much: 'How can a man be righteous before God?' (9:2). But Job's friends do not content themselves with this general statement. Instead, they accuse him of being a worse sinner than others. If he is suffering more than most, he must have sinned more than most. There is no other possible explanation: 'The light of the wicked indeed goes out, and the flame of his fire does not shine,' (18:5). 'Your light is going out Job; it must be because you are wicked.' 'The triumphing of the wicked is short, and the joy of the hypocrite is but for a moment,' (20:5). 'If your joy has gone Job it is because you are godless. All this piety that you have had all these years has been false. All this religion, all this sacrificing for your family, all these daily devotions, all this talk about communion with God—that is all it has been; just talk! Your joy is gone because you are godless.' Eliphaz becomes even more definite; 'Is not your wickedness great, and your iniquity without end?' (22: 5).

See how this works. The general statement that Job is a sinner is undoubtedly true; all men are sinners. But these men take an enormous step which seems to them to follow naturally, but which is not justified by the evidence. It is, in fact, quite wrong. They charge Job with being a worse sinner than others: that, they explain, is why he is suffering more than others. But **then** they take a further step which is even more serious: they go on to charge Job with specific sins.

Job has oppressed the poor and left them destitute, Zophar says. He accuses him of seizing houses he did not build, (20:19). Eliphaz adds in chapter 22 'You have taken pledges from your brother for no reason, and stripped the naked of their clothing. You have not given the weary water to drink, and you have withheld bread from the hungry. You have sent widows away empty and the strength of the fatherless was crushed,' (22: 6,7 and 9). These are very specific sins. In an Eastern culture, where hospitality is a prime virtue, they are very serious accusations to make about someone. His friends think they are fully justified though: 'Therefore snares are all around you, and sudden fear troubles you, or darkness so that you cannot see,' (22:10,11).

But Job is not guilty and he denies those specific sins. Listen to how his defence is translated in the NIV: 'Whoever heard me spoke well of me, those who saw me commended me, because I rescued the poor who cried for help and the fatherless with none to assist him. The man who was dying blessed me, I made the widow's heart sing. I put on righteousness as my clothing, justice was my robe and my turban. I was eyes to the blind and feet to the lame; I was a father to the needy, I took up the case of the stranger. I broke the fangs of the wicked and snatched the victims from their teeth,' (29:11-17). 'I was a good man,' says Job; 'I didn't do those things. I did the very reverse. Nobody ever went away from me needy. If I found somebody oppressed, I took on the oppressor, not the oppressed.' In chapter 31 he has to defend himself against the charge of sexual immorality (v.1). Job is not merely righteous on the outside, he knows the danger of thoughts; anticipating the teaching of Jesus by many centuries, Job refuses even to look lustfully at a woman (31:1, see the words of the Lord Jesus in Matthew 5:21-30).

What evidence do his friends have of such serious wrong-doing? None at all! There was not so much as a rumour about these things –and yet these men were so certain. Why is that? It is because they had made up their minds; here was a man who was suffering more than most so he must be a bigger sinner than most. Everybody knows what sin is, so they spell it out, but their accusations are no more than guess-work.

Eliphaz, however, claims not to be guessing; he claims that God has told him what Job has done. Did you notice that in chapter 4? 'In disquieting thoughts from the visions of the night, when deep sleep falls on men, fear came upon me, and trembling, which made all my bones shake. Then a spirit passed before my face; the hair on my body stood up. It stood still, but I could not discern its appearance. A form was before my eyes; there was silence; then I heard a voice....' (13-16). How does Eliphaz know that Job is guilty? 'I've had a revelation, you see; I have had a word from the Lord about this, Job.' What a great sin this is against Job. 'You shall not bear false witness,' is one of the commandments (Exodus 20:16). There are repeated warnings in the Bible against slander. There are warnings, too, against claiming that God has spoken when he has not: 'Woe to the foolish prophets who follow their own spirit and have seen nothing!... My hand will be against the prophets who envision futility and who divine lies.... I will cause a stormy wind to break forth in my fury; and there shall be a flooding rain in my anger, and great hailstones in fury to consume it,' (Ezekiel 13:3,9,13). Yet Job's friends persist with their slander and justify it by blasphemy! How dare they? How can they persist in such error? The truth is simple and shocking: they go on and on because they are men so gripped by what they consider to be the consequences of their theology that they are no longer able to think.

Is it wrong to be gripped by our theology? No, generally it is a good thing. Yet we have to be so careful; the straight statements of Scripture are true. 'Your word is very pure,' said the psalmist (Psalm 119:140). 'Your word is truth,' echoed Jesus (John 17:17). But the deductions we draw from Scripture may not be true and they may not be pure, because **we** are not straight. We are warped, we are fallen. Our reason, our discernment and our judgement are all fallen and so affected by sin. The deductions we make from Scripture and the systems we construct do not have the same authority as the Bible itself. For this reason we need to be humble and very careful, particularly in the judgements we make about others. God says to these friends at the end of the book 'My wrath is aroused against you' (42:7). That is a dreadful thing to hear! God is angry because they slander Job; his anger is all the fiercer because they claim that heaven has told them, but their tongues are set on fire by hell (James 3:6).

The first problem these friends have is that they have no sympathy with his plight; the second is that they make accusations with no evidence. We come now to the third problem and it is this: they refuse to accept that they may be wrong.

Trouble 3: They are over-confident

These men came to help Job. But when Job argues with them, and refuses to admit that he is 'guilty as charged,' that changes. They quickly move from wanting to help Job to wanting to prove that they are right. Their pride has become involved, and they want to win the argument. Because of this they cease to be humble seekers after truth, fellow sinners, bearing the burdens of Job and weeping with him who weeps. They do not carefully weigh up what is said and examine their own position. They are too proud to consider that they might be wrong.

As a result, they even begin to get angry with one another. In chapter 11, after the others have spoken to rebuke Job, Zophar turns on them. 'Should not the multitude of words be answered? And should a man full of talk be vindicated? Should your empty talk make men hold their peace? And when you mock, should no one rebuke you?' Zophar is angry. He is angry with Job for his 'empty talk' (verse 3) and his pride (verse 4). But he is also angry with the other friends because they have failed to prove their case, so he turns on them as well. He brushes them aside and ridicules them. Zophar is angry because he is proud; he wants to prove his case. To prove his case he is prepared to crush Job even further.

Trouble 4: They are undiscerning

The fourth mistake they make, and it is one of the biggest, is that they confuse a general truth with an absolute truth. It **is** generally true that the godly prosper. Certainly that is a recurring theme in the Bible. Think about the following verses. 'Blessed is the man who walks not in the counsel of the ungodly, nor stands in the path of sinners, nor sits in the seat of the scornful; but his delight is in the law of the Lord, and in his law he meditates day and night. He shall be like a tree planted by the rivers of water, that brings forth its fruit in its season, whose leaf also shall not wither; and whatever he does shall prosper,' (Psalm 1:1-3). 'He who would love life and see good days, let him refrain his tongue from evil, and his lips from speaking guile; let him turn away from evil and do good; let him seek peace and pursue it. For the eyes of the Lord are on the righteous, and his ears are open to their prayers; but the face of the Lord is against those who do evil,' (1 Peter 3:10-12). It **is** a general rule that those who are godly do prosper, and even the book of Job is in full agreement with that. Job was a godly man and at the beginning of his life he knew great prosperity. At the end of his life he knew even greater prosperity. It is only in this interlude that he suffers.

Many people have pointed out that the rise of Protestantism in Europe in the sixteenth and seventeenth centuries, and in particular the great influence of Calvinism, produced a very prosperous society and very prosperous men. That is just what the Bible would lead us to expect. Godliness does bring its reward; that is a general rule. But it is not an infallible rule.

It is a great problem to the writers of the Bible that sometimes the godly suffer. Psalm 73, for example, is a psalm telling one man's struggle with this truth.

'Truly God is good to Israel, to such as are pure in heart. But as for me, my feet had almost stumbled; my steps had nearly slipped. For I was envious of the boastful, when I saw the prosperity of the wicked. For there are no pangs in their death, but their strength is firm. They are not in trouble as other men, nor are they plagued like other men.... Surely I have cleansed my heart in vain and washed my hands in innocence. For all day long I have been plagued, and chastened every morning.' (Psalm 73:1-5, 13-14)

Job's friends would not have understood this problem. For them, there are no exceptions; the godly prosper and sinners suffer. But there **are** exceptions to this rule. The Lord Jesus Christ himself is an exception. If these three men had gathered at the foot of the cross, who do you think they would have blamed for what was happening? Jesus himself! We can almost hear them: 'You must be suffering dreadfully up there, but of course you have brought it on yourself . The Bible says, 'Cursed is everyone who hangs on a tree.' God has cursed you; you must have done dreadful things to deserve it.' But they would have been wrong. There is a mystery to the sufferings of Jesus that was not fully revealed at the time. Men considered him stricken by God, smitten by him and afflicted, and they were right. But they did not understand he was not pierced for his own transgressions, but for ours.

There is in fact no simple equation linking sin and suffering—but there is a natural tendency to say that there is. I call it 'Sound of Music theology,' and it does keep rearing its head. Do you remember the song from the film? 'Nothing comes from nothing, nothing ever could. Somewhere in my youth or childhood, I must have done something good...' Life is not as straightforward as that song implies.

The Lord Jesus Christ destroys that simple equation for his hearers. In Luke 13 he refers to some of the hot news of the day. There had been a great massacre when Pilate had murdered some Jews and mixed their blood with that of the temple sacrifices. It was a great sacrilege, and the talk of the nation at that time. How could God have allowed it to happen? Surely, the victims must have been great sinners! That is what people were beginning to say, but Jesus answers, 'Do you suppose that these Galileans were worse sinners than all other Galileans because they suffered such things? I tell you, no; but unless you repent, you will all likewise perish.' Then Jesus refers to another great disaster of the day:

'Or those eighteen on whom the tower in Siloam fell and killed them, do you think they were worse sinners than all other men who dwelt in Jerusalem? I tell you, no; but unless you repent, you will all likewise perish,' (Luke 13:4,5).

He makes the same point again in John's Gospel: 'As Jesus passed by, he saw a man who was blind from birth. And his disciples asked him 'Rabbi, who sinned, this man or his parents, that he was born blind?" Here is a New Testament example of Job's comforters! The disciples are asking themselves exactly the same questions and getting exactly the same answers. For them, this is not a man with a severe handicap; it is a problem in moral theology! He was born blind and blindness is a result of sin. Whose sin is it? That is their dilemma. It could not be the man's **own** sin if he were born blind, but on the other hand it could not be the sin of his parents. No man is punished for the sins of his parents. 'This is a problem Lord,' they say in effect. 'Tell us the answer: how do you bring the equation to bear on this instance?' But the Lord's answer would have taken them by surprise. 'Neither this man nor his parents sinned,' he said. He does not mean of course that they had never sinned; but he does mean that it was not their sin (parent or child) that had brought about this blindness. 'But [this happened so] that the works of God should be revealed in him,' he says, and then he goes on to heal the man's blindness (John 9:1-4). The Lord Jesus is teaching a great truth: often there are other explanations for suffering. That might raise some other questions for us: why should God cause a man to be born blind, and to grow up blind simply in order that Jesus can show his power? But that is what Jesus says, and we must trust God and accept it.

So the Lord Jesus severs the links in the chain that his disciples are determined to make. We cannot measure a man's godliness by his prosperity, nor can we judge his sin by his suffering. We have no right to look at those who are suffering badly and say 'Well they must have done something to deserve it.' (Of course they have; they have done something to deserve hell; and so have we.) Yet this reaction will not go away, and I have heard Christians who were mature enough to know better say exactly that. 'God must be very angry with them,' they say—as if there were no book of Job in the Bible.

We can understand what is going on in the minds of these three men of course; they are feeling very threatened. If Job has not brought this on himself, the whole moral fabric of their universe collapses around them. Even worse, if Job has not brought this on himself, they are not secure themselves. If God can do this to a man who has not done anything to bring it on, then he can do it to them as well. Job charges them with that fear in 6:21. 'You see terror,' he says 'and are afraid.' Fear often makes us strike out at others, and that is just what they are doing. 'I have to believe that you brought this on yourself, otherwise I would be afraid because it could happen to me.'

Trouble 5: They are ignorant

The final mistake that we are going to look at in this chapter is that Job's friends think they know more than they do. They think they know all the factors that are involved here. Suffering is caused by sin; Job is suffering; Job must therefore be suffering for his sin. There is nothing else involved.

Actually, they are very ignorant; there are many things they do not know. In particular, they do not know about the heavenly conference and so are ignorant of the confrontation between God and Satan. They do not know about the spiritual battle in heavenly places.

Not only do they not know it now, Job does not know it either, and neither the friends nor Job ever find out about it. Job is never told what has happened, or why these things have happened to him. It remains a mystery to him and his friends. The friends are ignorant—and they are ignorant of their ignorance!

We must recognise that these friends are actually part of the Satanic attack. Satan's attack does not end when Job takes ill. Satan's purpose, remember, is not to deprive Job of his health and his wealth; it is to make Job curse God. These friends are Satan's masterpiece. It is hard for anyone to maintain their godliness when people come up to them and say, 'If you were really godly you would be able to take this suffering without a murmur. If you were really godly it would not have happened to you anyway.' It is harder still to maintain godliness when accused of very specific sins without any evidence. Satan is still working on Job; he is still trying to bring Job down. He is relentless; these friends just will not let go. On and on they go, chapter after chapter and speech after speech. Behind it all is the relentless malevolence of the Evil One. How horrified the friends would be at the idea; but it is true.

It is part of Satan's strategy to use believers against one another; we have seen that he even tried this strategy against the Lord Jesus. The Bible says 'Faithful are the wounds of a friend,' (Proverbs 27:6), but how much grace it needs to remain friends with someone we wound. Often it is easier to be friends with someone who has wounded us. It can be quite easy to forgive them, particularly if we can see that it is justified. How much harder it can be though when we need to rebuke someone else, to retain our respect for them and our love for them as a person. Yet once we lose that love and respect, our ability to help them shrivels. Job's friends could not help him, once they had dismissed him as a gross sinner.

Job's friends fail here and Satan gets in. Because they think they know all the factors involved they use their theology to attack Job. It is a good thing to know our Bibles, and it is a good thing to know the system of theology that the Bible teaches. (It does teach a system!) It is very dangerous though when we begin to think that everything is simple. That is the trouble; a fascination with theology can make us arrogant. 'Knowledge puffs up,' (1 Corinthians 8:1). Without love, we become a sounding brass, a clanging cymbal.

What have we learned so far in the book of Job? We learned in the first chapter that God is in control. We saw in the second chapter that there is a heavenly dimension to events on earth, which we may know nothing about, but which have a very real impact on what is going on. Now I hope we have learned in this chapter that things are not as simple as they sometimes seem. To feel that quickly quoting a text or a sweeping application of a theological truth answers our problems is a sign that we are still babies spiritually; worse still, it makes us not just useless as counsellors or friends, but positively dangerous. We need maturity to realise this, before we give counsel to others. The Scottish preacher George Philip comments 'The difference between God's dealings, whether direct or by human instrumentality, and the dealings of men who are not moved by the Spirit of God is that **God wounds and in the process makes you whole.** When he makes you sore it is to bind you up, but men wound you and leave you with gaping sores and throbbing bruises. There is something quite demonic about man's inhumanity to man...'[1]

Chapter 3 Note

1   **George Philip,** *Lord from the depths I cry.* Gray.

Where there's smoke...

Please read Job chapters 4 -31

Where there's smoke, there's fire, they say. Is it true? We need to look in this chapter at the reality of innocent suffering. It is a crucial subject both for the book of Job and for our own contemporary situation. Because it is so important, I am asking you to read rather a lot of the book of Job for this chapter; you might find it helpful to read these chapters one 'round' at a time, as indicated below.

We have begun to see that Job's three friends repeatedly insist that the sole reason for his suffering is that his sin has caused it. They had no idea that a truly innocent man could suffer. We have seen a little of their reasoning, and some of Job's answers to that. Now we will follow both their reasoning and Job's answers more closely.

It is a very relevant topic in our own day; a form of teaching has become popular again which we can call prosperity teaching; prosperity teachers claim it is God's purpose that all God's children should be healthy and wealthy (not wise as well apparently—perhaps that would be too big a miracle?) If Christians are ill or poor they are falling below God's best for them; something therefore must be wrong with their faith. It is a very persistent idea and some will go to great lengths to defend it. Some years ago I picked up a new commentary on Job whose author insisted that, all through the years, the church had misunderstood the message of the book of Job; the friends were right and Job was suffering because of his sin! And this in spite of the fact that, both at the beginning and end of the book, God makes his own, very different, verdict clear. (See 1:8 and 42:7,8.) Later we will try to see where such teachers get their ideas from, and to answer some of the points that they make; but first, we must look at these three rounds of speeches. Beginning in chapter 4, the speeches continue until the end of chapter 31. Each friend makes a speech in turn; Job responds to it, and then it is the turn of the next friend. There is considerable overlapping so, to avoid repetition, I have tried to isolate the main element in each of the speeches.

The first round: chapters 4-14
Eliphaz

The main thought of this first round is a basic one: 'You are a sinner Job.' Eliphaz begins this with a great call to Job not to despise the Lord's discipline. In verse 17 of chapter 5 he says, 'Happy is the man whom God corrects.' At this particular moment Job is very far from being happy! The NIV more helpfully translates it 'Blessed,' and the difference is helpfully expressed by John Blanchard, commenting on the beatitudes ('Blessed are...'): 'Blessedness is related not to emotions but to character. When the Bible tells us that someone is 'blessed' it is not telling us what they feel but what they are.... Happiness is a subjective state, whereas blessedness is an objective state.'[1] And he goes on to quote John Stott: 'The Beatitudes are not an indication of their feelings but a declaration of God's assessment of them.' That is helpful for us, because this is undoubtedly what Eliphaz would have had in mind here. 'Happy (blessed) is the man whom God corrects; therefore do not despise the chastening of the Almighty.' This is a true and necessary comment, and it is taken up in Hebrews 12:5: 'My son, do not despise the chastening of the Lord, nor be discouraged when you are rebuked by him.' Often in a believer's suffering there is this element: the chastening, the discipline, of the Lord. But the fundamental assumption of Eliphaz is wrong: 'Who ever perished being innocent?' George Philip comments, 'We could trace the answer to that from Abel in the book of Genesis to the martyrs in the book of Revelation.' And he is right; all the way through the Scriptures, the innocent suffer. The Scriptures are very realistic and describe our own very real world. Surely we must say in response to Eliphaz, 'If this is discipline, something has gone wrong. Job is not being disciplined here; he is being crushed.' Discipline is a good and necessary thing, even though it never seems pleasant at the time; we believe in discipline. But there must be an element of *proportion* in discipline; we believe in disciplining our children, but we don't chop off their heads for spilling their dinner! Something has gone badly wrong when discipline is out of proportion; and unless God is no longer dealing with Job in grace, and hell has started for him, this cannot be discipline.

Bildad

In his speeches, Bildad appears as a hard man to like. In effect, Bildad says, 'Your children got what they deserved, but if you are innocent, God will deliver you,' (see 8:4,6). Put yourself in Job's position for a moment. Your children have been taken from you at a stroke, and your pastor comes round to see you. What words of comfort or strength does he bring? 'They deserved it you know,' he says, 'but if you are righteous, God will bring you through.' That is not helpful pastoral counsel! Some Christians seem to want to give the impression that they know all there is to know about God, and are not prepared to leave any mysteries. It is frightening the way they think they have God all neatly taped; they think they can say how God is going to react in every given situation. Aldous Huxley once said 'I cannot stand Christians; they know too much about God,' and there is a sense in which he is right. Beware of being a Bildad!

Zophar

Then Zophar steps in. 'Actually Job, you are not getting all you deserve,' he says (see 11:6). 'Know this,' he continues, 'God has even forgotten some of your sin. If God were giving you everything you deserve, you would be far worse off than this.' There is just enough truth there to make us shudder. There is a sense in which that is true (because we all deserve hell) but that is not what Zophar means; he still has his mind on the quite straightforward (to him) connection between earthly sin and earthly misery: '[If you] would not let wickedness dwell in your tents, then surely you could lift up your face without spot... and your life would be brighter than noonday...but the eyes of the wicked will fail and they shall not escape,' (11:14,17,20). Remember, Zophar is wrong. He does not know what he is talking about; he does not know about the godliness of Job, and he does not know about that counsel in heaven.

Job's reply

Job replies to each of these men individually; he does not wait until they have all had a turn. But for convenience we will collect his responses together. There are many things that Job says that deserve attention; in particular, his understanding of God's greatness and wisdom (9:2-10), his strength and justice (9:19) and his sovereignty (12:13-25) is exemplary. Though Job is bewildered and distressed beyond measure, he has not forgotten what he knows about God. Nor has he lost his confidence in God, for he says 'Though he slay me, yet will I trust him,' (13:15)—a trust we will examine later. In that trust, though, Job is sure that his friends have got it wrong. His replies to them have three elements.

First, he says 'You cannot actually convict me of sin.' He throws down a challenge which he knows they cannot meet, though they do try! 'Teach me and I will hold my tongue; cause me to understand wherein I have erred,' (6:24). 'Unless you can prove your case,' he says, 'shut up! Unless you can tell me what I have actually done, it is time for you to be quiet.' So far they have spoken only in generalisations, and he demands that they be specific. It is easy to blacken the reputation of a godly man with general statements and sly innuendoes; but what has Job actually done? As we saw in the last chapter, and will see again in the next few pages, Eliphaz is eventually provoked to answer this dishonestly, by inventing specific sins that Job must be guilty of.

Second, Job goes on to say, 'How can a man be righteous before God?' (9:2). He admits that, in the ultimate sense, no-one is truly righteous in God's sight; this truth, which the friends enunciate, Job agrees with. It is even true of the friends themselves, he points out: 'Will it be well when he searches *you* out?' (13:9, emphasis mine). Job does not claim to be perfect at all, anywhere in the whole book. He does not say 'I have never sinned and there is nothing wrong with my nature at all.' He knows his only plea with God is for mercy, (see 9:15). But he does insist, repeatedly, that 'My sins do not explain my suffering.' He is, though, prepared to be convinced if he is wrong, and he cries out to God, 'Make me know my transgression and my sin. Why do you hide your face?' (13:23,24). If all this is my fault, Lord—show me!

Then in 9:33 he cries out for a mediator: 'If only there were someone to arbitrate between us, to lay his hand upon us both, someone to remove God's rod from me, so that his terror would frighten me no more,' (NIV). Job is not afraid of meeting with God. His friends are saying 'You need to be careful; God is going to come down to you if you are not careful' and Job says 'Good! I want to meet with God, I want to ask him what is going on, I want to know what is wrong.' But he is aware that for this, he needs a mediator. Why does he need that? Campbell Morgan put it like this: 'How can a man argue his case with God so as to justify himself? His friends had declared that he was suffering on account of sin. His inquiry was as to how he could argue his case with God, so as to prove that this accusation was false.... The cry of Job was born of a double consciousness which at the moment was mastering him; first, that of the appalling greatness and majesty of God; and secondly, that of his own comparative littleness. This was not the question of a man who had dismissed God from his life and from the universe, and was living merely upon the earth level. It was rather the cry of a man who knew God, and was overwhelmed by the sense of his greatness.... Over against that was the sense of his own comparative smallness. He felt he could not get to this God. He was altogether too small.' [2] He is not afraid of God's presence, he is not hiding some secret sin in his heart. He knows that he is innocent, and he is quite willing to declare his continued innocence; but he needs someone to be a go-between. We can only note in passing how well that plea is answered in Christ, someone who can '...lay his hand on us both.' That is the marvel of the God-man, the one mediator between God and man. Christ, who is God and stands on equal terms with God the Father, and yet is a man who can stand on equal terms with us. He lays his hand on us both.

But if Job is aware that he is too small to answer God, he has no reservations about answering his friends. 'Men at ease have contempt for misfortune,' (NIV) he says; it is easy to speak when you are at ease. Job mocks their wisdom and their assurance. 'No doubt you are the people, and wisdom will die with you!' he says. 'Even the beasts of the earth could tell you that you are wrong,' he continues (see 12:7-9) 'and I myself am not inferior to you when it comes to knowledge,' (13:2). 'But talking to you is pointless; I would speak to the Almighty,' (13:3,4).

The second round: chapters 15-21
When Job's friends realise that they have failed to persuade him, they

come back for another try. The main thought of the second round is that only the wicked perish; having failed to make their case against Job in the first round, the friends step back a little to prove their case from this wider generalisation.

Eliphaz

Eliphaz and friends now appeal back *from* the particular (you are a sinner Job and that explains everything!) *to* the general (everybody knows that when anyone suffers it is a result of their sin) in order to prove their case. Smarting from Job's insult, Eliphaz appeals to the authorities: 'Are you the first man who was born?...Have you heard the counsel of God? Do you limit wisdom to yourself?... Both the grey haired and the aged are among us, much older than your father.' Eliphaz is charging Job with arrogance; the aged, wise and learned men, he insists, are on his side. He goes on to argue that the wicked may prosper temporarily, but judgement is lying in wait for them. 'Though he has covered his face with his fatness, and made his waist heavy with fat, he dwells in desolate cities, in houses which no-one inhabits, which are destined to become ruins.' In ancient days in the East, to be fat was seen as a blessing. It was regarded as a sign of prosperity, and as a sign therefore of God's blessing. That is the point of Eliphaz' insistence, 'Though he has covered his face with fatness... he will not be rich, nor will his wealth continue.' You have prospered temporarily, Job, but you are not going to do so any longer!

Bildad

In **his** second speech, Bildad tries to be reasonable, and appeals to Job to do the same. 'Gain understanding,' he says in 18:2, 'and afterward we will speak.' And he goes on to complain against Job for treating his friends as no wiser than animals (18:3, see 12:7-9) and expecting 'the universe to be turned on its head simply for his own benefit,' as Derek Thomas puts it in his commentary on verse four. [3] It is self-evident, continues Bildad, 'The light of the wicked (and, by implication, only the wicked) indeed goes out,' (v 5). He explains wickedness then in a very vivid picture; when a man behaves wickedly, he sets traps which eventually catch the man himself—a net, a snare, a noose. These traps inevitably lead to the wicked man's own destruction, and his case then becomes an example and a warning for men all over the world (see verses 8-21).

Zophar

Zophar's second speech contains very little that is original. He takes up the idea of the inevitability of the wicked being brought down; he may triumph—but only for a short time (20:5). He may find evil sweet in his mouth, but it will be sour in his stomach—in fact, cobra venom (20:12,14)! There is no ultimate escape; if the wicked man does manage to avoid one form of judgement, another one will catch him: 'He will flee from the iron weapon; a bronze bow will pierce him through,' (20:24). It will be a case of 'Out of the frying pan, into the fire,' he says. 'It is drawn, and comes out of the body; yes, the glittering point comes out of his gall. Terrors come upon him; total darkness is reserved for his treasures. An unfanned fire will consume him; it shall go ill with him who is left in his tent. The heavens will reveal his iniquity, and the earth will rise up against him. The increase of his house will depart, and his goods will flow away in the day of his wrath. This is the portion from God for a wicked man, the heritage appointed to him by God,' (20:25-29). No wicked man prospers for ever; this explains everything about Job, as far as Zophar is concerned.

Job's reply

Once again, we will consider Job's three responses together. In chapter 16, he begins by mocking his friends; miserable comforters he calls them, with words of wind. If their positions were reversed, he says, he would try to strengthen and comfort them; he would try to relieve their grief, but they merely shake their heads at him, (v 1-5). Then he goes on to assert his innocence: 'No violence is in my hands and my prayer is pure,' (v 17). In effect, he takes an oath on that by appealing to heaven itself: 'Surely even now my witness is in heaven, and my evidence is on high,' (16:19,20). While the friends are sure that God is punishing him for his sins, Job is not afraid to cry to God for vindication; his conscience is clear and he can draw near to God without fear.

He takes that theme up again in chapter 19. Verse 25 is surely the most well-known verse in the whole book, so memorably set to music by Handel. It is a flash of lightning in Job's darkness which really marks the centre of the book: 'I know that my Redeemer lives, and he shall stand at last on the earth; and after my skin is destroyed, this I know, that in my flesh I shall see God.'

Next, Job tells his friends that what they are saying is nonsense: everybody knows that the wicked flourish, 21:7. 'Why do the wicked live and become old, yes become mighty in their power? Their descendants are established with them in their sight, and their offspring before their eyes.' ('Unlike me,' he is saying, 'I have had my children taken away from me.') 'Their houses are safe from fear, neither is the rod of God upon them. Their bull breeds without failure; their cow calves without miscarriage.' This is the true experience of the world, he says; wicked men prosper. Here, Job is at his bluntest: 'How can you comfort me with your empty words?' (verse 34; the NIV reads 'console me with your nonsense'). Everybody knows you are talking rubbish, he says.

The third round: chapters 22-31

But if Job is not persuaded by their arguments, neither are the friends persuaded by his, and so they come back at him with a third round of speeches. This time, we can probably best summarise the speeches in the simple words 'We can prove it!' Let us begin with Eliphaz, as he speaks of the sins he is sure Job has committed.

Eliphaz

Eliphaz has not moved very far; he reiterates his conviction that Job's sins have brought this disaster on him, though this time he introduces more than a note of sarcasm: 'Is it because of your fear of him that he reproves you and enters into judgement with you?' (22:4). Perhaps he is here reacting to Job's assertion that 'everyone knows' the wicked prosper. 'Is it then a proof that you are holy, now that you are suffering Job? Is that what you mean?' Then Eliphaz takes a daring and inexcusable step: he declares that he knows, not only that Job has sinned, but also which particular sins Job has committed; he begins to charge

Job with specific sins. He charges Job with demanding security from his brothers for no reason, stripping men of their clothing and leaving them naked (which is specifically forbidden in God's word: see for example Exodus 22:26), giving no water to the weary, withholding food from the hungry, sending widows away empty handed, breaking the strength of the fatherless and, in general, oppressing the poor. Now Eliphaz is right that such things are very serious sins: speaking to the rich who have oppressed the poor, James writes 'the wages of the labourers who mowed your fields, which you kept back by fraud, cry out; and the cries of the reapers have reached the ears of the Lord of Sabaoth,' (James 5:4). But where has Eliphaz got the idea that Job has done this? Where is his evidence? Who has Eliphaz been talking to? The startling answer is: nobody. This has never happened. But Eliphaz is so sure of his case that he invents the sin. He ignores the fact that bearing false witness is certainly sin too; indeed, he would surely have dogmatically declared that he was not guilty of that. Of course Job must have done these things! Notice how he tries to prove his case; not by bringing a witness but by simply stating in a very dogmatic fashion what he believes Job to have done. 'You **have** taken pledges from your brother for no reason... you **have not** given the weary water to drink... you **have** withheld bread from the hungry... you **have** sent widows away empty' (verses 6,7,9). Such sins are literally godless; they come from a belief that there either is no God, or that if God exists he does not see or care what happens. This is what Eliphaz says next, 'And you say, 'What does God know? Can he judge through the deep darkness? Thick clouds cover him so that he cannot see," (verses 13,14). The psalmist speaks of that same attitude in the prosperous wicked when he says, 'They say, 'How does God know? And is there knowledge in the Most High? Behold, these are the ungodly," (Psalm 73:11,12). So Eliphaz not only accuses Job of unrighteousness, but of ungodliness; yet it is Eliphaz himself who has a tongue 'set on fire by hell,' (James 3:6).

Bildad

In his third speech, Bildad seems to have run out of things to say; he merely repeats that God is great, and a mere man cannot truly be righteous before him. As we have said before, this is true enough, and Job himself has agreed with this; but it is not what is at issue here. At least he does not go so far as Zophar and invent things; instead he simply repeats his pious platitudes in the hope of seeming wise. He would have been better advised to keep quiet, for 'Even a fool is counted wise when he holds his peace; when he shuts his lip, he is considered perceptive' (Proverbs 17:28).

And in fact, that is precisely what Zophar does; he has no third speech at all, and it is the wisest thing he has done!

Job's reply

As the friends continue to attack Job with their words, his spirits sink. Already reeling at the horrific onslaughts of the devil, Job now finds his trust in God has almost reached breaking point. Earlier, he had said 'Though he slay me, yet will I trust him,' (13:15); now he feels that God has abandoned him. Everything is more confused than it ever has been. Wisely, he does the only thing that he can do; he hangs on to what he knows, and reaffirms his integrity. 'Till I die I will not put away my integrity from me... My heart [used here in the sense of conscience] shall not reproach me as long as I live,' (27:5,6). At this point in his experience Job has become unsure of almost everything. We can imagine that his mind is in a whirl and he hardly knows how to go on answering his accusers, or what to say to his own doubts. But there is one thing he does know, and he takes his stand there. Sadly perhaps, it is not the faithfulness of God that he takes his stand on at this point; he is too low for that. Indeed, he feels that 'God... has taken away my justice' (27: 2). But he does know his own righteousness, and there at least he can stand. It is a very low level; it might strike some readers as unspiritual; but the point is, he does take a stand! The great preacher Martyn Lloyd-Jones makes this point: 'I do not care very much where we take our stand, so long as we take it; I do not care how low our stand is, so long as we are standing and not sliding. It is better to stand on the lowest rung of the ladder than to be down in the depths. Now this man started at the very bottom, and from there he began to ascend.' [4] Lloyd-Jones is commenting on Psalm 73, but his words apply equally well to

Job here. This is the only firm ground Job can find, and he takes his stand on it. 'I know I have not done any of these things,' he says, 'and nobody, NOBODY is going to bully me into saying that I have. I am not guilty,' he says, 'of the sins you have charged me with.' He then begins to spell out his innocence; he is not guilty of sexual immorality, and does not even look lustfully on women: 'I have made a covenant with my eyes; why then should I look upon a young woman?' Then 'I am not guilty,' he says (31:5) 'of falsehood. I am not guilty of adultery (31:9). I am not guilty of injustice (31:13), I am not guilty of materialism (31:24), I am not guilty of hard-heartedness (31:29ff). I have not done any of these things.'

We began this chapter with the question: is it true that there is no smoke without fire? Do the righteous suffer, or not? Yes they do; from Abel in Genesis to the martyrs in Revelation, the righteous often suffer. That is the general case, but what about the specific? Is Job suffering because he is wicked, or not? The answer to that must be clear to anyone who reads the book at all; it is a resounding 'No.' We have followed the friends as they try to prove their case; we have followed Job as he denies their case. But we do not only have Job's estimate of his own character; we have God's estimate of that character as well. We have seen God challenge Satan: 'Have you considered my servant Job that there is none like him on the earth, a blameless and upright man, one who fears God and shuns evil?' (1:8). That verdict is confirmed at the end of the book when God says to Eliphaz, 'My wrath is aroused against you and your two friends, for you have not spoken of me what is right, as my servant Job has... my servant Job shall pray for you. For I will accept him, lest I deal with you according to your folly...' (42:7,8). So both at the beginning and at the end of the book, God testifies to Job's goodness, to Job's integrity, to Job's blamelessness.

Suffering is a mystery; we have not seen yet in Job any answer as to why God allows suffering. But we have seen one very important question answered: Does suffering prove that we are worse sinners than others? No; it may well indicate the very reverse. God knew he could trust Job, and knew that Job would not buckle under pressure. When God trusts us to suffer, when he wagers (as it were) his reputation upon us, it may well be a sign of his trust in us. It may be that through our difficulties and sufferings he is accomplishing things we cannot even know. We can certainly know, though, that God's word is true, and that however great our sufferings may be, they are part of the 'all things' that work together for good to those who love God (Romans 8:28). God has a plan for the world, and a victory over Satan and the forces of darkness to win. We have a part to play in that, and must look with confidence to that day when his victory is finally manifest, when heaven has arrived and there is no more sorrow, nor crying, nor pain. In the meantime, there **is** often smoke without fire.

Chapter 4 Notes

1   **John Blanchard,** *The Beatitudes for today.* Day One.
2   **Campbell Morgan,** *The answers of Jesus to Job.* Oliphants.
3   **Derek Thomas,** *The storm breaks.* Evangelical Press.
4   **D.M. Lloyd-Jones,** *Faith on Trial.* IVP.

Healthy, wealthy and struggling?

Please read Job chapter 15 and 1 Corinthians 15:50-58

Bill Pethybridge of Worldwide Evangelisation Crusade was due to speak at a church on the far side of London; he could afford to get there, but had insufficient money to get back. Confident that the Lord would provide, he went to the church, spoke, and then hung around as unobtrusively as possible waiting for some angel of the Lord to slip him some money or offer him a lift. He waited—and waited; and eventually everyone had gone. Finally, standing all alone, he said, 'But Lord, you promised to supply all my needs,' and felt that the Lord was responding, 'That's right, and you need exercise. Start walking!'

As Christians we believe that the Lord has promised to supply all our needs; that is what the Scripture says (Philippians 4:19), and many of us have clear and precious testimonies to the way the Lord has done exactly that. But increasingly in recent years voices have been raised to suggest that we are not taking God seriously enough; that God wants all his people to be healthy and wealthy. So our cities host big campaigns which no longer simply promise eternal life to those who repent and believe. In addition, they now promise that those who arrive in wheelchairs will be able to walk home; those who arrive with cancers will be healed and that no problem, particularly no health-problem, is too big or intractable. The full gospel will sort it out. God's healer is in town; he's done wonders for people just like you, and all you have to do is come along, bring your faith, and you too will be healed.

The view that suffering and sin are always linked has been around for a long time, as we have seen. We have noted it already in the so-called 'comforters' who came to Job; and we noticed as well that it did crop up in the ministry of the Lord Jesus. On one occasion the disciples spoke to him of a blind man, blind from birth, and asked, 'Who sinned, this man or his parents, that he should be born blind?' (John 9:2). Some of the rabbis said that sin was linked to suffering; others quoted examples of those who were born suffering to prove them wrong. Then the response would come back 'Ah, but the parents..' and the debate went on. So the disciples, knowing that Jesus would have the definitive answer, asked him 'Who sinned, this man or his parents?' In reply, Jesus said, 'Neither this man nor his parents sinned that he should be born blind...' With one phrase, Jesus severs the link. The same problem recurred in the case of the Galileans who died when the tower fell on them, (Luke 13:4). 'Do you think they were worse sinners than others? I tell you, no...' And yet, in spite of this, the myth persists.

Often, however, it takes a slightly different form, that goes like this. 'Sin and suffering—whether illness or poverty or whatever—**are** infallibly linked. Some Christians still get ill because they haven't recognised the link. They don't recognise that, now they're part of God's new kingdom, they can have all they want from God. It's just a matter of faith: didn't Jesus say, 'according to your faith be it unto you?' and doesn't the Bible say, 'He took all our sicknesses...?' Christians need to be delivered from this lack of faith, and enter into the health and wealth that God has for them.' So Colin Dye writes, 'Every blessing that God has for us **on the earth** has already been accomplished on the cross of Jesus Christ...' and goes on to write of a woman named Sue, who 'began to lay claim to physical healing believing that Jesus paid for it on the cross.... Once we see what by faith is available to us we will never settle for anything less than God's best for every area of our lives. We will want to go on to possess all the spiritual truths and practical realities which God has given to us. That's breakthrough faith.' [1]

This teaching is sometimes known as the 'prosperity gospel'. It has many advocates (particularly in the United States) but it is a basic misunderstanding of the Christian faith. The whole emphasis of this movement is fundamentally anti-gospel.

Its attractiveness

Of course, the idea that we can have whatever we want, and have it now, is an attractive idea. For one thing, we live in a consumer-crazy society, where we are told that what we want we can have, and straight away. In addition, we are repeatedly urged to believe that we have lots of rights but no real duties. Small wonder that many are taken in by promises of a God who is Santa Claus to the millionth power! And, of course, when we are in financial trouble, or when we or those we love are ill, we do call to God for help. Rightly so: but it seems only a small step to believing that God is bound to help.

Its failure

But sadly, this teaching fails. It does not work because it is not true. Take the matter of healing, for example: Professor Verna Wright lists at least seven surveys of claims to healing. Some of these were done by Christian groups and others by secular medical groups; and Wright concludes, 'All the detailed analyses which have been made of healing claims over the years have failed to produce evidence of cures being achieved except for the kind of disorders which in medicine we call **functional** states.'[2] (That is, those which—while real—are known to be susceptible to suggestion.)

Its cruelty

There are times when this doctrine is extraordinarily cruel; imagine, for example, telling the parents of a dying boy that, if only they had enough faith, he would be healed. It is also very dangerous; Verna Wright tells of two cases of people known to him who died as a direct result of believing that God had healed them—because they were assured that God always heals those who have the faith.

When we first moved to Aylesbury, my wife began to visit Stoke Mandeville Hospital with a Christian group who were leading worship for the patients. Stoke Mandeville Hospital is world famous for its spinal injuries unit. There are some very tragic cases in there; many people, young and old, who have been left paralysed after accidents. In the end, she had to give up. Why? Because again and again, these seriously disabled people were being assured that, if only they had faith, they could get up from their wheel-chairs **now** and walk away **now**. Of course, if they were still in their chairs at the end of the evening, it wasn't the evangelist's fault, was it? Oddly enough, these people with shattered spines were being told these things by men who wore glasses! Where was **their** faith, we wondered?

Dishonouring the Lord

Many people who have never heard the term 'prosperity gospel' or of any of its advocates still nonetheless fall into similar errors. I recently heard Dick Lucas of St. Helen's Church, Bishopsgate describe a time when he preached to a group of eminent surgeons, not all of whom would have been Christians. He spoke of their reaction to his describing a scene in the consulting room: the surgeon has just, with tenderness and concern, done the most difficult job he ever has to do and told the patient that there is no hope. Death is not far away. Then the enthusiastic Christian patient, instead of reacting with shock, smiles and says, 'Don't worry Doctor; God has told us he is going to heal. Medical science can do nothing; now God is free to act.' What interested me about Lucas' description was what he said of the attitude of the surgeons: at this point, you could hear a pin drop. It was clear that many surgeons had come across just that response. But let us not deceive ourselves: these patients then die; their families suffer all the normal pain of bereavement but compounded by an immense turmoil of faith. Among unbelievers, the gospel is dishonoured.

Christ has defeated death but the full results of that victory only show in him. They do not yet show for us. Our victory over death must wait until Christ returns, as Paul tells us in 1 Corinthians 15:22,23. He goes on to say in verse 24 that the Lord is currently destroying dominions and authorities and powers, but that the last enemy to be destroyed will be death (verse 26). That does not mean there is no foretaste of that victory for us; there is—its sting has been removed (verse 56). As a result, Christians down the ages have been able to face death with confidence. But that is not the same as being delivered from death itself.

Verna Wright quotes several very sad examples of the failure of this teaching, from the student who had been 'cured' of a very heavy cold but complained 'the devil is keeping the symptoms there' to the lady who insisted that she had been cured of rheumatoid arthritis at a large holiday convention, even though her hands were still gnarled and deformed. These all add to my conviction that many Christians are dishonouring the Lord by claiming what is not true. No doubt that dishonour is unintentional, but it is very real.

What are they saying?

Perhaps you have never come across some of the more extreme 'Bible teachers' who are contributing to this confusion. Let me give you some quotes from some of them, just enough to give you an idea of what is being claimed.

American 'word faith' teacher Kenneth Copeland had an extract from his television program shown on the BBC in which he said, 'When sickness and disease tries to attach itself to our bodies, NO! That didn't come from God. He bore the curse so I could bear the blessing. Hallelujah! So I'm not going to receive that; I reject it, I resist it—and the Bible says resist the devil and he will flee from you.' On the same television show his wife Gloria read Deuteronomy 28:11. In the version she was reading it said, 'The LORD will grant you a surplus of prosperity,' and she commented, 'That's the Lord's plan for you—not just getting by!'

In much of this thinking God becomes no more than a mere machine to satisfy our whims: Robert Titlon claims that God is already committed to his part of a strange covenant relationship with us. We can make whatever commitment or promise to him we want 'then we can tell God on the authority of his word what we would like him to do. That's right! You can actually tell God what you would like his part in the covenant to be!' [3] The same man says, 'Being poor is a sin, when God promises prosperity,' [4] and 'My God's rich! And he's trying to show you how to draw out of your heavenly account that Jesus bought and paid for and purchased for you at Calvary.' 'New house,? New car? That's chicken feed. That's nothing compared to what God wants to do for you.' [5] Again, he encourages people to make a thousand dollar vow to his ministry—especially if they cannot afford it—as a sign that they have faith God is going to make them rich. He says, 'I'm trying to talk you out of that dump you're in! I'm trying to talk you into a decent car!

... I'm trying to help you! Quit cursing me! Quit cursing me!'

And, talking of 'trying to talk you into a decent car', Roy Clements tells the story [6] of an advertisement sent to him that had particular relevance. The advertisement asked 'Why be trapped in a Datsun when you have a Daimler faith...?' At the time, Roy did drive a Datsun and, being six feet five inches tall, sometimes felt trapped in it! The advertisement went on: 'God wants every one of his children to prosper... He has promised to give you whatever you ask for in faith, so just 'Name it and claim it." It can be tempting, and Roy admits that he felt the temptation—until he opened his Bible and read 'In troubles, hardships and distresses; in beatings, imprisonments and riots; in hard work, sleepless nights and hunger... sorrowful, yet always rejoicing; poor, yet making many rich; having nothing, and yet possessing everything' (2 Corinthians 6:4,5,10, NIV).

Sadly, it would be possible to go on with a whole multiplication of quotations. Somehow, many today have reduced the whole concept of the infinite, eternal and sovereign God of the Bible to a God who is there to do our bidding; a radical reversal of the Christian teaching that we are here to do his bidding!

How these preachers use Scripture

But do these teachers have a case? They claim to be Bible teachers; what about the texts that they use? Are they right in teaching that Scripture promises health and wealth to all who have faith? Obviously, we cannot look at all the texts they may quote, but it will repay us to consider some of them.

One favourite text is Exodus 15:26: 'If you diligently heed the voice of the Lord your God and do what is right in his sight, give ear to his commandments and keep all his statutes, I will put none of the diseases on you which I have brought on the Egyptians. For I am the Lord who heals you.' It is obvious, is it not, that if it were God's will to heal the Israelites, it is his will to heal Christians today? No, not at all. That was a promise given to specific individuals at a specific time and was conditional on their obedience, and we have no ground for believing that that promise is applicable to us now. The New

Testament does not take up that verse and apply it to Christians at all.

More difficult to answer perhaps is the often-made claim that there is 'healing in the atonement,' which then quotes Matthew 8:16,17 as proof. 'When evening had come, they brought to him many who were demon-possessed. And he (Jesus) cast out the spirits with a word, and healed all who were sick, that it might be fulfilled which was spoken by Isaiah the prophet, saying 'He himself took our infirmities and bore our sicknesses.' Matthew here is himself quoting Isaiah 53:4, which reads in our translation 'Surely he has borne our griefs and carried our sorrows.' How are we to understand this?

The New Testament normally quotes Isaiah 53 with reference to our salvation—the way, in fact, that our translation translates Isaiah's words. What Matthew is doing in his Gospel is highlighting one particular thing; that through Jesus **all** the consequences of sin will be dealt with. Inevitably, that includes disease and sickness. Jesus' earthly ministry demonstrated that he had the right and power to remove sickness and disease from the earth; and the New Testament holds out the certain hope that one day they will be gone forever. This text is not intended to prove that no believer anywhere should ever get sick, and the rest of the New Testament makes this clear. When Timothy suffers stomach problems, Paul does not write, 'Grasp the meaning of Isaiah 53; Jesus has born your stomach-ache and you have no right to suffer it yourself!' Instead, he says 'Use a little wine for your stomach's sake and your frequent infirmities' (1 Timothy 5:23).

Of course there is a sense in which our sicknesses **are** dealt with at the cross. When Revelation 21:4 says that God 'will wipe away every tear from their eyes; there shall be no more death, nor sorrow, nor crying; and there shall be no more pain, for the former things have passed away,' it is describing one of the effects of Calvary. Once in heaven, we will find that, in a very real sense, the death of Jesus did pay the price that freed us from **all** the consequences of sin, including sickness. But until then, we endure.

Another favourite verse of such teachers is John 14:12: 'Most assuredly, I say to you, he who believes in me, the works that I do he will do also; and greater works than these he will do, because I go to my father.' Rory Alec, presenter and head of Christian Television Europe, quoted in a BBC television programme the passage from Acts (19:12) about Paul's handkerchief being taken to heal the sick. Immediately afterwards he quoted these words of Jesus as if they imply that Paul could do that, so we are going to do even greater things. That hardly needs a biblical refutation. Why not? Because of what John 14:12 actually says. It does not say, 'Anyone who believes in me ought to be doing these things and is only failing to do them because they don't have enough faith.' It says, unconditionally, 'he who believes in me, the works that I do he **will** do also' That ought to alert us to be careful about what Jesus actually means here. The traditional interpretation is the one that fits the facts best. Leon Morris explains it like this: 'What Jesus means we may see in the narratives of the Acts. There there are a few miracles of healing, but the emphasis is on the mighty works of conversion. On the day of Pentecost alone more were added to the little band of believers than throughout Christ's entire earthly life. There we see a literal fulfilment of 'greater works than these shall he do." [7] Certainly we must realise that even the apostles did not do greater **miracles** than Jesus did: he raised the dead and so did they; but he stilled a storm, and they did not. He rose from the dead himself, and they did not. Morris therefore also quotes Bishop Ryle, ' 'Greater works' means more conversions. There is no greater work possible than the conversion of a soul.'[8]

A child of the age

This whole prosperity gospel teaching is very much a child of the age we live in. We are in an age which wants everything, and wants it yesterday. Nobody waits for anything anymore; we no longer save up for new furniture, we put it on Visa. Why should we wait for all our diseases to be dealt with? We want it now! And the unfaithfulness of today's church to the word of God, and the consequent decline in her influence and power, has made us all long for better days. It is not too surprising if some take a wrong turn. But it **is** a wrong turn: New Testament Christianity does not promise us everything we could want now. Liberalism tries to persuade us to live **below** the gospel, below the Scriptures, but this enthusiasm tries to persuade us to live **above** the Scriptures and to claim things that are not yet ours. There are things we may experience now; but there are other things which have a 'not yet' about them. Full health is one of them.

The cross: our true pattern

Perhaps the problem can be helpfully put like this; these teachers tell us that we must live in the light of the resurrection. All God's power is being made available to us and we need to appropriate resurrection power. But in the New Testament it is the cross, rather than the resurrection, that is the model for Christian living. Jesus said that if we were not prepared to take up our cross daily, we could not be his disciples (Luke 9:23). The cross speaks of death, not resurrection power. Paul writes like that about his own life and ministry: we always carry around in our bodies the death of Jesus, he says (2 Corinthians 4:10). When he goes on to speak of the life of Jesus being revealed, he says 'death is working in us but life in you.' Again, he says of himself 'even to the present hour we both hunger and thirst and we are poorly clothed' (1 Corinthians 4:11). **The** evidence of resurrection power in the life of the believer, according to Paul in Philippians, is that we share in his sufferings (Philippians 3:10).

Perhaps I may illustrate from my own life in a way that every Christian should understand. There have been two major miracles in my life: the **first** is the one that plucked me from a life of godlessness and turned me to God, plucked me from sin and washed me clean, took me out of the Kingdom of darkness and placed me in the kingdom of God's own dear Son. The **second** miracle is the one that has kept me, and keeps on keeping me, there! For the Christian life is not always easy, and my own flesh reacts against its discipline; and yet, by grace, here I am. And you too; if you are a Christian, you have known the same two miracles.

There is, of course, more to come. But it is 'not yet'. There are things which we cannot have now **not** because we do not have enough faith, but because God reserves them for the life to come. We cannot have 'heaven on earth'—we must wait for 'heaven in heaven'. I am not saying that there is nothing on earth for Christians but trouble and strife and difficulty. If I said that it would be false; there are many blessings God gives to his people. But you may remember Churchill's famous words to the House of Commons in May 1940, 'I have nothing to offer but blood, toil, tears and sweat.' They have their parallel in Christian experience. Dick Lucas points out, 'The proper vocabulary to use about abundant Christian living is toil, stress, pressure, weakness.' Those words are in 1 Corinthians! We are in a battle; we must fight; and it is not going to be easy. Godliness is not a way to worldly gain -see 1 Timothy 6:5-16. As Roy Clements comments: 'Great men and women of God do not pray for Daimlers; they pray for endurance.' [9]

And that is the point of 1 Corinthians 15:50-58. The Corinthian church, too, had become caught up with the kind of misunderstandings that we have been considering. One of the major reasons Paul wrote to them was to call them back from that. His conclusion is magnificent, but to many Christians today it would seem an anti-climax. The Corinthians have got so caught up with wisdom and miracles and other things that have only been a distraction for them. What do they need to hear? What do **we** need to hear, as we live lives that are not always easy, as we press on and seek to serve the Lord? What is the message about the power of God in our lives that Paul wants them and us to know? 'Be steadfast, immovable, always abounding in the work of the Lord, knowing that your labour is not in vain in the Lord' (1 Corinthians 15:58). **Is** this an anticlimax? By no means! How we need to be a people that are 'immovable'. We have the gospel, the power of God for the salvation of all those that believe; we cannot move from it. In particular we dare not move from it in pursuit of an illusory dream of health and wealth. Rather, we need to resolve that while we have life and breath, we will abound in the work of the Lord.

Surely the greatest evidence of the power of God in the world is to be found in the saints who have suffered and triumphed. It is no coincidence surely that the two best-known women in the Christian world today are Joni Eareckson and Elizabeth Elliott—both of whom have ministries that have been shaped by suffering. How do you explain their lives? The power of God.

One final story to make the point. Alison MacKay was a Christian, and a pastor's wife, who died on 27th December 1995 of cystic fibrosis. She was just twenty-eight years old, and she left a husband and a son of five. Knowing she was dying, she said goodbye to her son in memorable words: 'Bye-bye now James. Remember that you must follow Jesus. In life the important thing is not to be rich or happy: it's holiness.' How can we explain such a conversation in such circumstances? The power of God. That is the kind of power I yearn for, and the Saviour I yearn to serve—a Saviour who produces such love, grace, and peace in the very face of death. Yes, I believe that we need to see more of God's power, and I believe that it is available. But it is this kind of power we need, the power for godliness in adversity.

Chapter 5: Notes

1   **Colin Dye,** *Breakthrough Faith.*
2   **The Healing Epidemic,** *Peter Masters and Verna Wright.* Wakeman.
3   Quoted in **John MacArthur,** *Charismatic Chaos.* Zondervan.
4   **ibid.**
5   **ibid.**
6   **Roy Clements,** *The Strength of Weakness.* Christian Focus.
7   **Leon Morris,** *The gospel according to John.* Eerdmans.
8   **Ibid.**
9   **op. cit.**

The Pilgrim's Progress

Please read Job chapters 6,7,9,13,17 and 19

William Carey had been in India nearly twenty years. He had a heart burdened to reach the Indian people with the gospel and was tireless in his work towards that end. Though not regarding himself as particularly gifted, he had mastered several languages, started up a printing-press to publish Bibles in the native languages, and was making considerable progress toward his dream. Then, on March 11th 1812, a fire swept through his printing works. Almost everything in it was destroyed; the loss in paper alone was immense. Carey recorded, 'In one short evening the labours of years are consumed. How unsearchable are the ways of God! I had lately brought some things to the utmost perfection of which they seemed capable, and contemplated the missionary establishment with perhaps too much self-congratulation. The Lord has laid me low, that I may look more simply to him.' Carey and his associates buckled down to work, and wrote in 1825, 'The New Testament will soon be printed in thirty-four languages, and the Old Testament in eight, besides versions in three varieties of the Hindustani New Testament.' Carey stands for us as a true example of faith, trusting God when everything seems calculated to bring us to despair.

In this chapter, we will examine the character of Job's spiritual life and see how he fares under the trials that come to him. I have called the chapter 'Pilgrim's Progress' because that is what we will see: a real man, brought very low, but beginning at last to climb again. Do read the chapters I have listed at the beginning of this chapter; as we look at extracts from them we will see true faith beginning to triumph over doubt and fear.

1. Self-pity

Undoubtedly, Job's immediate reaction to his trials is one of self-pity. This is well expressed in chapter 6 verse 2, 'Oh, that my grief were fully weighed, and my calamity laid with it in the balances! For then it would be heavier than the sand of the sea.' Job describes very honestly for us just how he feels. One of the great things about the Bible is just how honest it is! The characters we see in it are not plaster saints, immune from normal human reactions. They are real people; people who hurt, who fail, who complain and then people who rise in faith to the God they serve. This passage is important because real living faith in God does not always triumph immediately.

Some Christians never seem to be troubled by anything. They never have doubts, they are never cast down, they are never spiritually low. Somehow they just seem to shrug off troubles and trials—especially those of other people! 'Well, you know you should just be trusting God,' they say. 'Dear me, how can you be so low, how can you let things get you down, how can you weep so much? Don't you believe God?' Such a person is not spiritual, but just insensitive; nothing could be further from biblical faith than that. It is a great mistake when Christians try and emulate such a person. I remember a minister describing a funeral he had conducted. It was a Christian who had died, and the whole family were Christians too; it seemed to them that grief would indicate a lack of faith and so they were determined not to show any. But he had to say to them, 'You know, you can cry. It's all right to grieve—God doesn't mind. It isn't spiritual to stiffen the upper lip and to carry on as if there was no problem and no grief.' Job did not make that mistake; but it was a mistake to let grief become self-pity.

It may well have been the attitude of his friends that pushed Job from grief into self-pity. 'I'm not crying without cause,' he reminds them in effect—and that is certainly true. He has suffered enormously, and what miserable comforters these friends are. He describes them in graphic terms in verses 14-30 of chapter six. 'My brothers are as undependable as intermittent streams,' he complains (verse 15, NIV). We can easily understand the imagery he is using. Though water is available for us at the turn of a tap, in a desert travellers rely on the known courses of streams to find their refreshment. We can well imagine what it must be like when they find that a stream has dried up. 'I was looking to you for refreshment,' he says to his friends; 'but you are like intermittent streams: dry just when you are most needed.' He goes on, 'To him who is afflicted, kindness should be shown by his friend, even though he forsakes the fear of the Almighty' (6:14). Even if Job were guilty of great sin, he would still need friends. Only by demonstrating the depth of their love and care for him would they be able to reclaim him.

Christians often need to take this to heart. It is too easy, when our brother begins to wander, for us to retreat from him immediately as if he had some contagious disease. Sadly, many Christians find themselves wandering in a spiritual wilderness for prolonged periods just because, when they began to suffer or to wander, no-one cared enough to understand. 'Where were you,' says Job, 'when I needed you?'

Perhaps you know the Yorkshire proverb that 'a friend in need is a real nuisance.' Is that not how we feel sometimes? But real friendship should not be like this. The friendship of David and Jonathan is one of history's greatest friendships, and the Bible carefully records for us how Jonathan tried to help David when David was in trouble. Jonathan's father Saul was king, but God had appointed David, not Jonathan, to succeed Saul. Although Jonathan knew this, he warned David that Saul was trying to kill him (1 Samuel 19:1). He interceded with his father on David's behalf (19:4) and even risked his own life to arrange David's escape (20:35). On one very difficult occasion, this great friendship is summed up with the words, 'Jonathan... went to David in the woods and strengthened his hand in God' (1 Samuel 23:16). Jonathan is a clear example of the love Paul describes in 1 Corinthians 13: 'Love... does not envy; love does not parade itself, is not puffed up; does not behave rudely, does not seek its own, is not provoked, thinks no evil, bears all things, believes all things, hopes all things, endures all things' (4-7). Job's friends show a complete absence of such love.

2. Anger

In chapter 7 Job turns away from his friends and turns on God himself. **First,** he argues that life itself is pointless (1-10), **then** he complains that God will not give him rest even at night (11-16) and **finally** he admits the reality of his sin, but asks what difference that can possibly make to God.

Life is pointless

'My days are swifter than a weaver's shuttle and are spent without hope' (7:6). A weaver's shuttle moves at quite a speed; Job's life is going like that too. Life does go by quickly, for 'all flesh is grass, and all its loveliness is like the flower of the field. The grass withers, the flower fades, because the breath of the Lord blows upon it; surely the people are grass' (Isaiah 40:6,7). But to Job, it seems even worse than that. His days are spent without hope and life seems pointless. It is as if the weaver's shuttle is still moving at its accustomed speed, but the thread has run out! The activity continues, but nothing useful is produced any longer.

God gives him no rest

Job is having trouble sleeping. When his day just becomes too wearisome to continue he seeks refuge in sleep. 'I say, 'My bed will comfort me, my couch will ease my complaint'' (7:13). But sadly, it does not work; it seems to him that God is tormenting him even in his sleep. He is troubled by dreams and visions which scare him to the point that 'my soul chooses strangling' (verse 15)!

What difference could sin make?

Finally in this chapter, Job argues that his sin cannot possibly make any difference to God. 'Have I sinned? What have I done to you, O watcher of men?' (verse 20). His thought seems to be, as George Philip puts it, 'If I have sinned, what harm have I done? You are too big, God, to be hurt by a puny man like me, and in any case, since I am a burden to you and to myself, why not be done with me?' For that moment, he has lost sight of the fact that all sin is actually a rebellion against God himself, an offence to his holiness and inevitably therefore deserves **and** incurs God's wrath.

An emotion too far?

Obviously, Job is going too far; his distress is making him strike out and say things that ought not to be said. In his anger, he has turned on God himself. This is not a model of how we are to deal with God, or of how we are to approach him when things go wrong; but it does at least have the virtue of being honest. Job is real with God; he does not pretend. He does not cover his emotions with pious words. There is no hypocrisy here and that is good; one thing we know for sure is that God hates hypocrisy. 'When you pray,' said Jesus in a different context, 'you shall not be like the hypocrites,' (Matthew 6:5). The first epistle of Peter insists that we are to lay aside 'all malice, all guile, hypocrisy, envy and evil speaking' (2:1). Job knows of God's attitude to hypocrisy too, as he reveals in chapter 13: 'He also shall be my salvation, for a hypocrite could not come before him' (verse 16). Whatever sins Job is guilty of, hypocrisy is not one of them. The Greek word which is translated 'hypocrisy' in our New Testaments originally had to do with an actor, someone who was playing a part written for him but did not, obviously, really mean the words. Far too many prayers are just like that!

Far be it from any of us to encourage others to a wrong anger against God in their prayers. But do note that, at the end of the book when God appears to Job, Job is not condemned for this. God does not rebuke Job for having grown angry.

The same thing is illustrated in the life of Jeremiah. Jeremiah had been promised (Jeremiah 1:6-10) that when he preached, it would be with divine authority. But Jeremiah does not feel that this promise has been fulfilled; as the **New Bible Commentary** puts it, 'With reason, Jeremiah feels that there has been to date little compelling authority in what he has said from the Lord. People are amused but not convinced. The great promises appear as deceitful bait to lure him into an office he never desired.' It is a bold man who accuses God of deceit! Yet Jeremiah is not cast off as a result. The great thing about both Job and Jeremiah is that their prayers are real. They are in anguish, and it shows. George Philip comments, 'It may surprise some people to know that the saints at prayer are not always as serene as they are in a public prayer meeting.' He is right! And I, at least, do sometimes feel that **some** emotion in our prayer meetings would be an infinite improvement! Better the honesty of a Job or a Jeremiah than the rather bland prayers that usually characterise our meetings, which so often seem to say, 'Well here's my prayer, but really it makes very little difference to me or anybody else whether you answer it or not.' We may be absolutely sure that God prefers Job's honest, heartfelt emotion.

3. Terror

By the time we reach Job chapter 9, Job's reverent fear of the Lord has turned to abject terror. Perhaps that is because his friends insist that Job's sin has caused his problems; if they are right, then there may be much more to come. Job has not confessed his sin, he has not turned from his sin, he does not even know what his sin is; so if God is punishing him, he has probably only just begun! Job has allowed to take root within himself the idea that God is out to destroy him and so he is afraid to lift his head in case he is hit again. The New International Version helpfully translates 9:28 like this, 'I still dread all my sufferings...' showing us clearly that Job has possible **future** sufferings in mind. 'What on earth will God do to me next?'

A stern, unfeeling judge?

Satan often tempts us to see God as a stern and unfeeling judge, who is just looking for an excuse to send another thunderbolt to strike us. Nothing could be further from the truth.

It is true that we cannot trifle with God's holiness. Those who wilfully sin, and continue in it though often reproved, may be suddenly cut off without remedy. (See Proverbs 6:15 and 29:1.) Paul writes to the Corinthians and warns them against taking the Lord's Supper without examining themselves for sinful attitudes, and says 'For this reason many are weak and sick among you, and many sleep (that is, have died)' (1 Corinthians 11:30). Let me recount a 'real-life' incident.

As a young Christian I attended a young people's house party led by several young men from a church in the north of England. Shortly after the house party one of those young men left his wife to set up home with another woman, all the while continuing the routine of his Christian life: preaching, praying publicly, leading the church. He was then visited by a pastor, who made no claim to the gift of prophecy, who warned him: 'Brother, unless you repent, God will deal with you very severely; he will not allow his name to be defiled like this.' I think that it was within forty-eight hours that this young man was working under his car when the jack snapped and the car wheel crushed his head. 'Our God is a consuming fire.' (Hebrews 12:29). It is undoubtedly right to warn those who claim to be believers and are deliberately walking in known sin. We dare not try to play with God. The Acts of the Apostles records for us the sobering story of Ananias and Sapphira, suddenly struck dead by the Holy Spirit for their sin.

But it is not true that God waits to torment those who honestly and sincerely walk before him in love and faith. In the light of Calvary, where God so clearly demonstrates his love for us, how can we ever doubt it? We must never let Satan tempt us into a terror of God.

4. Looking outside himself

Just a few verses later, in 9:33, Job's head does begin to rise. Once more, I quote from the text of the New International Version, which helps us to see Job's progress more clearly. 'If only there was someone to arbitrate between us, to lay his hand upon us both, someone to remove God's rod from me, so that his terror would frighten me no more.'

One of the most remarkable things about the book of Job is to see how aware he is, all the way through, of some of the great doctrines of theology. Unbelieving scholars sometimes tell us that there is no doctrine of the afterlife in the Old Testament; but it is there in Job, as we shall see. In fact, many of the great doctrines of Christian theology are quite clearly known and assumed not only by Job but even by his friends as well. We have seen how, in the second verse of chapter 9, he punctured Bildad the windbag with just one question, 'How can a man be righteous before God?' When Bildad accuses him of being a sinner, Job responds by reminding them that it is not possible to be anything else!

Now, having given voice to the despair that many of us may feel when we contemplate God as a judge, Job begins to look outside himself and towards God for help. **First** he declares that he is unable to answer God himself. 'How then can I answer him?' he asks in verse 14 'and choose my words to reason with him? For though I were righteous I could not answer him; I would beg mercy of my judge; if I called and he answered me I would not believe that he was listening to my voice.' In other words, Job is saying that he cannot argue his case himself; 'I'm no great advocate,' says Job, 'I may have gifts, I may be able to speak, I may be able to present a case. But who can present a case like God? He knows all the ways of reason, he knows all about presenting cases in logical ways. Furthermore, he knows all about me, he knows what I'm going to say, he can anticipate my every argument. How could I stand before God? He is holy, I'm a sinner; he is in heaven, I'm on earth. I need somebody to plead my case. I need an advocate who can stand in the presence of God; I need someone to answer for me who is equal to God himself.'

Writing on this passage, Campbell Morgan says, 'the cry of Job was born of a double consciousness which at the moment was mastering him; first, that of the appalling greatness and majesty of God and secondly, that of his own comparative littleness.... To bring the idea into more modern terminology, it is as though Job had said: 'There is no umpire, there is no arbiter, there is no one who can stand between us, interpreting each to the other... Here then was Job crying out for some one who could stand authoritatively between God and himself.... Elemental humanity, aroused to a sense of the necessity for God, a consciousness that God cannot be reached, cried out for someone to stand between them. At last in clearest tones the answer is found in the declaration that such a One is found, 'the man Christ Jesus.' [1]

The important characteristic from this verse that I want to bring home to you is both exceedingly simple and exceedingly profound: Job's faith has begun to look outside itself. 'Look at yourself,' say the friends. 'Examine your heart and you'll know why you're suffering.' But Job answers, 'On the contrary; I have to look outside myself or I will never dare hope again!'

This is one of the first lessons we must learn: Christian faith is not a faith in ourselves. We do not hope in our own character, or our own goodness. We do not look to our own works for salvation, nor do we ever expect to find acceptance with God on the basis of what we are or have done. This is true of our salvation and it is also true of experience. There are times when, as the hymn-writer puts it, 'darkness seems to veil his face;' in such times, we can only experience hope if we can sing,

'I rest on his unchanging grace;
In every high and stormy gale,
My anchor holds within the veil.'

It is almost a truism to say that Christianity today has become very experience-centred. Too few Christians have learned to look at God and what he has done rather than at themselves and the way they feel. When things are going very well in their lives, they say they feel close to God. But then when things begin to get difficult for them, their faith is shaken; their faith is 'anchored' in their circumstances. But our spiritual anchor can only hold if it is 'within the veil', that is, if our hope is centred on objective facts about Christ and what he has done. That is well expressed by the same hymn writer, who continues:

His oath, his covenant, and blood
Support me in the whelming flood:
When all around my soul gives way,
He then is all my hope and stay.

His oath! We rely for our security on the fact that God has sworn on oath that his purpose will not fail, 'that by two immutable things, in which it is impossible for God to lie, we might have strong consolation, who have fled for refuge to lay hold of the hope set before us' (Hebrews 6:18). His covenant! Jesus is 'the mediator of the new covenant... that those who are called may receive the promise of the eternal inheritance' (Hebrews 9:15). His blood! For that covenant is sealed with the blood of the Lord Jesus and guaranteed by his resurrection from the dead.

Job has felt the futility and emptiness of looking to his circumstances; at last, his faith is beginning to climb. The next step will take him even higher.

5. Coming up...

Chapter 13 contains the very first high point of the book. After all his suffering, his doubts, and his complaints, Job's faith re-surfaces and he cries out, 'Though he slay me, yet will I trust him.' At last, real faith begins to triumph again. It is not very long since he was speaking of his dread of what God might still do to him (chapter nine) but now he has arrived at the point where he can re-affirm his trust. It is not that he is now convinced that God will do no more to him. The future is still unknown, just as the reasons for his current troubles are still unknown. What has brought about this change of heart?

There seem to be two things which Job speaks of in 12:13—that is, the wisdom and strength of God. Perhaps the constant foolish prattling of his counsellors has made him reflect not only on their lack of wisdom ('No doubt you are the people, and wisdom will die with you!' he says sarcastically in 12:2) but, by contrast, on the wisdom of God. 'With him [is] wisdom.' The word Job uses may speak of skill in war or in administration; the general idea is that God knows what he is doing! Job is certain that he does not understand what God is doing, and even more certain that his friends do not understand it either; but it is enough that God knows. Couple that with a realisation of God's strength, and Job is affirming that God not only knows what the wise thing to do is, but he has the power to do it as well. Job had always known this of course, but that knowledge seems to have been buried for a while. Now it surfaces, and brings with it a return of faith.

Ultimately, faith is not built on what God has done; it is built on who God is, that is, on the character of God himself. Satan's lie to God was 'Job only trusts you because you have made him rich.' But real faith trusts God because of the character of God; it trusts God because it knows that God is good.

Preaching on Psalm 106:1 ('Oh, give thanks to the Lord, for he is good,') Brian Edwards makes a helpful point, and it is worth quoting extensively.

'God does not need to do anything to be described as 'good.' We must understand that before we go any further. You see, we talk about a man and we say he is a good man, and the immediate response is, 'Why, what has he done?' That is the way we think, because we know that a man cannot be good in himself. He can only be good if he starts doing something; and of course, he will do a few good things here and there. But you do not talk like that about Almighty God. God was good before creation. God was good when there was nothing in existence—before space, before time, before eternity, when there was nothing but the triune Father, Son and Holy Spirit. God was good because he can never be anything else. He does not have to do anything to be good. He is good.'

It follows therefore, Edwards continues, that

'all his intentions and all his plans are good. The Christian starts there. God's power is never for evil; it is always for good. I do not understand all his ways. I do not understand what he is doing with my life sometimes. I do not understand what he is doing with other people's lives. There seems to be disaster upon disaster coming upon other people's lives. There seems to be problem upon problem. I do not understand all those natural disasters. I do not understand all those man-made disasters. I do not understand why God stands back and allows things to happen as he so often does, but I know his power is good. He can only **be** good, and he can only **do** good.' [2]

If we remember the foundation of the goodness of God it gives us somewhere to stand when things go wrong in our lives. We do not know why God does all he does; but once convinced of his goodness, we can trust him anyway. And when we consider our own sin, we realise that it is his mercies that are the mystery, not his chastisings. 'Though he slay me yet will I trust him.'

When everything is going well it is so easy to trust God; but that is not faith, it is sight. When things begin to go wrong, and we still trust him, that alone is faith. Christians sometimes sing a hymn by Horatio Gates Spafford:

'When peace like a river attendeth my way,
When sorrows like sea billows roll,
Whatever my lot, thou has taught me to say,
'It is well, it is well with my soul"

Spafford was a wealthy Chicago attorney in the last century; he was married with four daughters and one summer his wife and daughters set out to cross the Atlantic to Europe. Sadly, their boat was in collision with another, and sank; the four daughters all drowned. Mrs. Spafford was rescued and sent a tragic cable to her husband: 'All lost! I alone remain. What shall I do?' But while that was the worst of their tragedies, it was not the only one; for while they had been sailing there had been a bank crash in Chicago, and Spafford had lost all his wealth. His response was to write the hymn I have quoted above: 'When sorrows like sea billows roll... it is well with my soul.'

There are many such stories, some not nearly so well known. When Stephen and Margaret Marchant arrived in Austria in the early 1980s to begin missionary work, the first significant event was the death of their baby son. Many churches had been praying for them, and were deeply moved when they wrote home in the words of another hymn: 'He giveth more grace as the burdens grow greater.' That's faith.

God knows his man. God's reputation is safe with Job. Is it, I wonder, safe with us?

But Job's problems are not all solved; in chapter 17, he sinks again into despair.

6. ...and going down

'[God] has made me a by-word of the people... my eye has also grown dim because of sorrow.... If I say to corruption, 'You are my father,' and to the worm, 'You are my mother and my sister,' where then is my hope? ... Shall we have rest together in the dust?' (17:6,7,14,15,16). The upward climb of his faith is not a smooth one for Job, but this in no way invalidates the flashes of faith he has. It is very true to experience that there are times during our trials when God draws very close. Perhaps we are reading the word of God, or listening to a sermon, and we are suddenly aware that God is speaking specifically to us. It is so precious that we can almost laugh with our tears, and we cry out 'Yes, Lord, I do trust you.' But the trials have not disappeared, and the pain does not go away.

Let me illustrate again from our own experience. Back in the time of my wife's great illness, which I mentioned in chapter one, we knew what it was to be almost driven to despair. We began to wonder if God was telling us that we had missed our way and needed to get out of the ministry. (Now that we are less stressed, we do know that if he wanted to tell us that he would choose a different way!) One Sunday we were worshipping in a church far from home, where the preacher did not know us and certainly knew nothing of what we were going through. He was preaching on the text, 'Stand still and see the salvation of the Lord' (Exodus 14:13) when suddenly he paused and described, by way of illustration, a situation exactly like ours. We felt as if we were being held up for examination by the whole congregation! But we knew too that God was speaking to us; and when the preacher said, 'Don't be afraid; you have not missed the way. God wants you to wait for his timing, and then he will move you on,' we knew that we had heard God speak to us. It was very precious, and it did a lot to hold us in the months and years ahead. God had cared enough to answer our cry. But that answer did not make my wife Elaine well. It did not take away the pain and it did not eliminate the despair we felt at times.

So it was with Job; his progress was not a straight, upward line. So it is with all of us; faith may **rise above** emotion and despair at times, without having **conquered** emotion and despair. When we begin to sink again, we must not allow Satan to tell us that our faith was no faith, nor that the voice we heard was not God's voice. We are human still, and suffering hurts.

7. Assurance

Finally, what must surely be one of the high points in the Old Testament is reached in chapter 19 verse 25: 'For I know that my redeemer lives, and he shall stand at last on the earth; and after my skin is destroyed, this I know, that in my flesh I shall see God.' This is so important that we will give our next chapter to consider it in detail. But let us just note at this point that the afterlife is the ultimate solution to all our problems.

Job knew so much less about that afterlife than we do. God revealed more and more as time progressed, until the ultimate revelation came with our Lord Jesus Christ. In spite of this, Job still triumphs. He begins to look forward to that last great day of judgement, and so must we. 'After my skin is destroyed yet in my flesh I will see God, whom I shall see for myself, and my eyes shall behold, and not another. How my heart yearns within me.' He has begun not only to look to that day, but to yearn for that day. He knows that there is a redeemer. He knows that there is a resurrection for him, and that his body and his soul will be reunited. He knows that there is a day of judgement coming; those are the last words of chapter 19, as he warns his friends, 'That you may know there is judgement.' How his friends needed to know that. They had forgotten, and were sure all the answers must be in this world. They were wrong. How **our** world needs to remember this. There is a judgement coming. '[God] has appointed a day on which he will judge the world in righteousness by the man whom he has ordained. He has given assurance of this to all by raising him from the dead' (Acts 17:31). There is a judgement coming, and we will all stand before that throne. Job knows that Jesus will triumph on the earth; of course, he does not know the **name** of the Redeemer, but he knows the **fact** of the Redeemer. 'In the end, my redeemer will stand upon the earth.' He knows that the God who once walked with Adam and Eve in the Garden will walk on the earth again in triumph, having destroyed all his enemies—even the last one, death itself. Job begins to look to that day; he begins to look to heaven itself. It is a lesson that we all need to learn so that our faith may grow and triumph in times of despair.

Chapter 6 Notes

1   **Campbell Morgan,** *The answers of Jesus to Job.* Oliphants.
2   **Brian Edwards,** *God Cares.* Evangelical Press of Wales.

Lightning Flash!

Please read Job Chapter 19

'For I know that my redeemer lives, and he shall stand at the last on the earth; and after my skin is destroyed, this I know, that in my flesh I shall see God' (Job 19:25,26). This verse is undoubtedly one of the highest points in the Old Testament. In it Job, in the midst of his trials, his sufferings, his grief and his depression, suddenly declares his assurance that there is an afterlife and a resurrection, and that he will have a part in that. It is an amazing confession to find here for at least three reasons.

First because of the scale of Job's sufferings. Job believes himself to be on the edge of death—a very reasonable belief, since he is in fact very ill. All his family are lost to him; his children through death, his wife because she has turned against him. His so-called friends, from whom he might have expected a degree of devotion, have turned out to be miserable comforters, berating him and accusing him of sins that he has not committed.

Second because of the depths of his despair. Bewildered at the collapse of his world, Job has expressed his terror at being in the hands of a God who seems to have lost all sympathy for him. He is full of dread at what may happen to him next; but still, from somewhere, comes this flash of faith so bright it is like unexpected lightning on a dark night.

Third, because of the antiquity of the announcement. As I indicated in the first chapter, we do not know precisely when Job lived. The American Old Testament scholar E. J. Young reviews the evidence and concludes cautiously, 'It seems to me, therefore, that Job was probably a contemporary of the patriarchs...' [1] If he is right, then Job's declaration of faith dates from around 2000 BC! (True, Young and others believe that the book reached its current written form rather later; but provided we accept the reliability of the record, as Young himself does, that does not affect the date of the confession itself.) It is not unusual to be told by liberal or unbelieving scholars that there is no developed doctrine of the afterlife in the Old Testament—this statement alone shows them to be wrong. In fact, as we will see, many of the elements of the complete New Testament doctrine are already here, in embryo at least. It may be that Job did not understand all the implications of what he said—or, to put it another way, it is certain that he did not have all the light that we have on these truths; as W. H. Green comments '[a] wide chasm remains between those who preceded and those who followed the advent of the Son of God. The completed doctrine of Christ and the greatness of the redemption which he achieved, his own actual return from the state of the dead, and his ascension to heaven as the forerunner and type of his people, opened a new view and poured fresh light upon the mystery of the world to come.' [2] But Job plainly knew a great deal. In this chapter we will examine what he did know, and how the reality of that faith helped him.

1. Job knew his need of a redeemer

As we saw in chapter four, Job does not think he is without sin. In fact, he responds to the taunts of his friends by challenging them to answer, 'How can a man be righteous before God?' (9:2), and then goes on to remind them that this is true of them too: 'Will it be well when he searches you out?' (13:9). Job does not believe that his sins account for his sufferings; but he does not believe that he is without sin.

Nor is this just doctrine for him. The first chapter showed Job making sacrifices to atone for sins; it is the sins of his children that are mentioned, but we are not to think that he is ignoring his own sins. Job knew what the Psalmist would later declare and the apostle would stamp with his own authority: 'There is none righteous, no, not one' (Romans 3:10, see Psalm 14:3).

Then, we have seen him lamenting his **lack** of an advocate in 9:33, 'If only there were someone...' (NIV) and yearning for someone who is great enough to speak to God and yet human enough to intercede for Job; someone, as he puts it, 'to lay his hand on us both.' Now, as his faith begins to rise, he declares his conviction that he **does** have just such an advocate.

It is not the word 'advocate' that Job uses here however; it is the word 'redeemer.' In Old Testament times, a redeemer 'was a person's nearest relative... whose obligation could be to buy back family property... pay the necessary amount to save a kinsman from slavery... or to marry a widow and provide her dead husband with an heir... What this illustrated was that somebody had to pay a price to set free property from mortgage, animals from slaughter, persons from slavery or death, or the deceased from dishonour... Job is confident that such a redeemer exists who will defend his honour and integrity.' [3] Disowned by his friends, Job is now looking beyond them to one who will defend his cause and, ultimately, redeem him from death.

Job knows he needs a redeemer. He needs one who can buy back his life from the penalty of sin that he deserves. He needs one who can put things right between him and God, and he knows that he has such a redeemer. Nothing can be more urgent in this short, uncertain life of ours than that each of us too should be aware of that need. Arrogance will not diminish our need; we all fall short of God's standards and God's glory, and there can never be any hope for any of us except in a redeemer.

2. He also knew what kind of redeemer he needed

We dealt with this to some extent in the previous chapter, seeing how Job cries out for one who can bridge the gulf between him and God. At this point, let us spend a little time seeing just how perfectly the Lord Jesus Christ bridges that gulf.

Jesus is fully and completely God

Many of us are far too familiar with this truth to grasp how breathtaking it actually is! Once, in this earth of ours, there walked a man who looked like other men. He grew tired, like other men, and hungry like them too. There was nothing about his appearance to set him apart from others; so that when Judas agreed to betray him he had to say to the soldiers, 'The one I kiss is the one you want.' There was certainly no halo to mark him out! And yet, that man was truly God; not just 'a' god, or even 'divine' in some sense, but really and truly God, the maker of heaven and earth and all that is in them. 'In the beginning was the word, and the word was with God, and the word was God... and the word became flesh and dwelt among us, and we beheld his glory...' (John 1:1,14). While it is the common testimony of the New Testament that Jesus of Nazareth was and is God appearing in the flesh, the gospel of John makes it so clear in so many ways, we can safely confine ourselves for the purpose of this chapter to that one gospel. John tells us he wrote it 'that you may believe that Jesus is the Christ, the Son of God', and in it we see:

a) John's own conviction

By the time John, one of the original twelve apostles, sat down to write his gospel he had become fully convinced that his Master Jesus was God himself. He opens his gospel with a magnificent prologue in which he states this conviction clearly before beginning to marshal the evidence in order to convince us. Later, in chapter twelve of the gospel, John quotes Isaiah 6, where Isaiah saw the glory of Jehovah, and sees it fulfilled in the ministry of Jesus. A careful comparison of John 12:37,38 and John 12:41 will surely lead us to the conclusion that the NIV is quite right to translate verse 41 like this: 'Isaiah said this because he saw Jesus' glory and spoke about him.' There can be no doubt that John was convinced that Jesus was God.

b) Jesus' own claim

Then, John shows us Jesus claiming to be God in several ways. **First** Jesus claims eternity with the words, 'Before Abraham was, I am.' That is bad grammar in English; it is bad grammar in Greek too. But Jesus is making a point; the name Jehovah derives from the verb 'to be', and when Moses asked God, 'What shall I say when they ask me what your name is?' God replied 'I am who I am... say to the children of Israel, 'I am has sent me to you." (see Exodus 3:13,14). In using the words 'I am' of himself, then, Jesus was claiming to be God; the Jews knew this, which is why they tried to stone him. **Second** Jesus claimed to be one with the Father (John 10:30) and again the Jews recognised this as a claim to be God. Again they tried to stone him, but this time they explained it was 'for blasphemy, and because you, being a man, make yourself God' (verse 33). **Third** Jesus used the titles of God. For example, it is often overlooked that when Jesus said, 'I am the good shepherd,' the Jews would inevitably remember that Scripture says, 'The Lord (Jehovah) is my shepherd' (John 10:11 and Psalm 23:1). There can be no doubt that Jesus claimed to be God.

c) The disciples' own conclusion

From time to time those who were closest to Jesus must have asked themselves just who he was. Ironically, it was Thomas who got there first—ironically, because to this day we still call him '**doubting** Thomas.' After the resurrection, when Jesus appeared to his disciples, Thomas was not there; when they told him about it, he was adamant in his unbelief. 'Unless I see in his hands the print of the nails, and put my finger into the print of the nails, and put my hand into his side, I will not believe,' he said (John 20:25). A week later Jesus appeared again. This time Thomas was present, and Jesus invited him to do exactly what he had said: 'Reach your finger here, and look at my hands; and reach your hand here, and put it into my side. Do not be unbelieving, but believing' (20:27). It was at that point that the penny dropped for Thomas; now at last he really knew who Jesus was. 'My Lord and my God!' he cried out (20:28)—offering worship to Jesus which Jesus did not refuse. There can be no doubt that, in the end, the disciples came to the conclusion: Jesus was God!

Jesus is fully and completely man

At the time when the New Testament was being written, there was much wrong teaching about who Jesus was. Some of that teaching denied his deity, but some of it went in the other direction and denied that Jesus was truly a man. Some taught that he only **seemed** to be a man, but he had no real body. He was more of a phantom figure; if you had followed him through Palestine, you would have seen that he left no footprints in the sand. Various errors formed around this basic idea, but they are all condemned in the Scripture. 'Every spirit that confesses that Jesus Christ has come in the flesh is of God, and every spirit that does not confess that Jesus Christ has come in the flesh is not of God...

many deceivers have gone out into the world who do not confess Jesus Christ as coming in the flesh. This is a deceiver and an antichrist' (1 John 4:2,3; 2 John 7).

That Jesus was (and is) a real man is very clear from the pages of the gospels; he grew tired, he grew hungry. He knew what it was to be lonely, and he felt the need to pray. Though he had great powers, he said he could do nothing without his Father (John 5:19); though he had great knowledge, yet there were things he did not know (Matthew 24:36).

Everything that makes us human, Jesus had. (Of course, he had no sin; but it does not take sin to be human.) He was and still is a real man. But he also had everything that makes God, God. He was and still is true God of true God. This is a great mystery indeed (as Paul confesses, 'without controversy great is the mystery of godliness: God was manifested in the flesh...' 1 Tim. 3:16), but, mystery though it be, there could be no better answer to Job's cry for 'someone to lay his hand upon us both!'

How much of this did Job know? The answer is we just cannot tell. We do not know how much had been revealed, in Job's own day, about the coming incarnation because we are not told. There may have been much revealed and kept in oral form; but while we do not know how much Job knew, we do know that he knew what he needed. And what he needed is what we need; and the Lord Jesus Christ perfectly met his need and perfectly meets ours.

3. He also knew about the provision of a redeemer

Now that Job's faith has begun to surface again, it is vital to note that he did not just **hope** that there would be a redeemer; he knew that there was one. There is nothing surprising about this; faith is always built on revelation (Romans 10:17, 'Faith comes by hearing and hearing by the word of God,') and one of the very first things that God revealed to man after the Fall was of a coming Saviour. When he was pronouncing the curse on the serpent God said, 'I will put enmity between you and the woman and between your seed and her seed; he shall bruise your head, and you shall bruise his heel' (Genesis 3:15). This promise was the first time the gospel was ever preached and, though it was preached to Satan, the promise was given in the hearing of Adam and Eve. God declares that One will come who would be hurt by Satan, but would also crush Satan, undoing his works. Our first parents knew and understood that there had to be someone coming who would undo the effects of sin; and they were saved in the hope of that.

Undoubtedly, even before any Scripture was written down, the tradition that a redeemer would be provided would continue down the generations. Then, when Scripture began to be written, again and again the Scriptures pointed to the coming One. So full is the Old Testament of these promises that Jesus could say of the Old Testament Scriptures, 'these are they which testify of me' (John 5:39). This is how men and women were saved in Old Testament times; we are saved by looking back at what Christ has done on our behalf while they were saved by looking forward to what he would do for them.

Strangely, some Christians seem to have the idea that God has a 'try and try again' approach to salvation; that first he tried the law, and that failed, so then he tried the gospel. But that is not what the Scriptures teach; for example, the apostle Paul in Romans 3 and 4 goes to considerable length to show that Christians of his day were saved in exactly the same way—justified by faith in Christ—as Abraham and David had been in their day. Job too was saved in that same way—by looking to a redeemer. Here, he testifies to his knowledge of that coming redeemer.

4. Job knew about the resurrection life

'I know that my redeemer lives, and he shall stand at last on the earth; and after my skin is destroyed, this I know, that in my flesh I shall see God.' Job does not merely know that his redeemer lives; he also knows that he, Job, will live again and see the redeemer God in the flesh. Some commentators have argued that resurrection life is not in Job's view here but most evangelical commentators have always seen this verse as a clear, magnificent statement of faith in a coming resurrection, and I am glad to join them. See how beautifully and clearly he puts it: 'In my flesh I shall see God... my eyes shall behold...' Job knew about the resurrection life.

The 'facts of death'

We are used to hearing about 'the facts of life.' Much more important though are what we could call 'the facts of death.' What are they? They go like this. First, death is a judgement. It is not part of what we might call 'creation's natural order,' but it was introduced by God as a judgement on creation when Adam and Eve fell. Second, at death the soul of the believer enters heaven, for 'to be absent from the body is to be present with the Lord' (2 Corinthians 5:8), while that of the unbeliever goes to hell—see Luke 16:23. Third, once the soul has left, the body of believer and unbeliever alike begins to decay and may even be eaten by worms, as the more familiar translation (AV) of this verse says. But there is one fact about death that we usually forget; death is temporary. Contrary to all appearances, death is temporary. 'Do not marvel at this,' says Jesus, 'for the hour is coming in which all who are in the graves will hear his voice and come forth' (John 5:28). The Bible clearly teaches a universal resurrection of both good and evil alike. At the last day, body and spirit are reunited, and after that will come judgement. Job has at least a glimmering of knowledge of this, and speaks here of his confidence. 'After my skin is destroyed, this I know, that in my flesh I shall see God.'

The resurrection body

Very little is said in the Bible about the resurrection body of the wicked, but more is said about that of the believer. It is called a glorious body: '[he] will transform our lowly body that it may be conformed to his glorious body,' we are told (Philippians 3:21). It is called a spiritual body (1 Corinthians 15:44): that is, it has not so much of the earth and no decay or corruption about it. Corruption came in as a result of the Fall, and is completely absent from the resurrection body. Paul admits that he does not know too many details of what this body would be like, just as we could not guess from the seed of wheat that is sown what the body of wheat will be like (1 Corinthians 15:35-44). But he does know, and so should we, that God can do what he wants, and he rhapsodises in expectation of that glorious, coming, resurrection body.

5. Assurance

We end this chapter where we ended the last one, noting Job's assured conviction of these things. There is more here than guesswork, and more than hope; we are not reading this magnificent text properly unless one word is in capital letters: 'I KNOW that my redeemer lives.' The dark night of the soul has been very dark indeed for Job, and it is not over yet. But for one brief moment his darkness is illuminated with this brilliant flash of light, like a lightning flash, as Job rejoices not just that there is a resurrection, but that he has a redeemer. Where does that assurance come from?

The nature of faith

The first thing we have to say about assurance is that it belongs to the very nature of saving faith. Because true faith is trust in God, rather than in oneself, an element of assurance has to be there. We have seen how Job began to look again outside of himself and up to God; it was almost inevitable that, as he did so, assurance would surface, riding on the crest of his faith.

The work of God

Do you remember that when Peter finally realised who Jesus was, the Lord said to him, 'Flesh and blood has not revealed that to you, but my Father who is in heaven' (Matthew 16:17)? Up until that point there had been great discussion among the disciples as to who, precisely, their Lord was; but now, Peter has this sudden assurance, and he blurts out the answer. That, says Jesus, is the work of God in your heart. True assurance always is. Grudem puts it helpfully,

'The Holy Spirit bears witness 'with our spirit that we are children of God' (Romans 8:16), and gives evidence of the work of God within us: 'And by this we know that he abides in us, by the Spirit whom he has given us' (1 John 3:24). 'By this we know that we abide in him and he in us, because he has given us of his Spirit' (1 John 4:13). The Holy Spirit not only witnesses to us that we are God's children, but also witnesses that God abides in us and that we are abiding in him. Once again more than our intellect is involved: the

Spirit works to give us assurance at the subjective level...as well.' [4]

However, believers do not always experience unbroken assurance; that much must be clear from Job's earlier experience. But no believer should be satisfied without it. This witness of the Spirit is more than an important doctrine; without it, faith can be lifeless, unattractive and hardly able to stand in the evil day.

The marriage picture

I am sure we all know of marriages which are sadly just marriages in contract only. For whatever reason, there is no longer any tenderness between the husband and the wife. Often even outsiders cannot avoid picking up the vibrations; something is wrong. There are other marriages though where there is still great love, tenderness and even passion. It is not necessary to witness that love and tenderness and passion being expressed to know the difference; there is just a reality about some marriages. When you are with them, you know you are in the presence of a couple who care for each other.

There are Christians whose walk with God is like that first sort of marriage. It is real no doubt; they really are united to Christ. But for some reason there is no longer any joy in it. There is no passion in it, and no tenderness. They know they are saved and can tell you the date when it happened. That is, of course, good. But there are others who know they are saved because today the Lord came to them again and showered his love upon them. Their walk with God still has tenderness, it still has passion. Although Job's faith has been shaken, although he has been walking in darkness, at this point God comes to him, and touches him, and faith bursts to the surface.

How does this assurance help Job? His sufferings are not taken away, his depression does not disappear. It does not solve the problem of God's dealings with him. But this understanding of immortality does help Job's inner turmoil, and bring him to realise that there is peace between himself and God which outward trials cannot destroy. He is no longer tormented by a sense of God's hostility and wrath, even though his outward situation is unchanged.

Job suffered more than most, and he still stood and triumphed. The way to stand when trials come is to live the life of faith. Live in such a way that the clean Spirit ('clean' is the word for 'holy' in some languages) is not grieved and may take up full abode within. Job lived such a life; we have God's testimony to that. It is when we are that sort of believer that, in the times of our darkness, trials and distress, God will suddenly touch us; the fireworks explode in our souls, and our souls cry, 'I know that my redeemer lives.'

Chapter 7 Notes

1   **E.J. Young,** *An Introduction to the Old Testament.* Eerdmans.
2   **W.H. Green,** *Argument from the Book of Job.* Klock and Klock.
3   **Derek Thomas,** *The storm breaks.* Evangelical Press.
4   **Wayne Grudem,** *Systematic Theology.* IVP.

Hell has a fury

Please read Job chapter 21

Is there an answer to the problem of suffering? We have seen Job descend into a deep pit of despair, and we have begun to follow him too as he climbs out. But we have not had suffering explained to us yet. The insistence by his friends that Job is suffering because of his great sin is refuted by every speech Job makes, as well as by the book as a whole; but the problem remains. Why is life so unfair?

So much suffering

Perhaps for most of us, when we were very young it did not seem to be too much of a problem. By nature, I suspect most of us are rather like Job's friends! We see people around us with their difficulties and their distresses, and we recognise that their lives are not totally happy; there are very real problems. But it is all too easy to suspect that, somehow, it is all their own fault. We are sure that life will not be like that for us. We will find the perfect partner, we will have the perfect marriage and two point four almost-perfect children. We will join the right church and serve God publicly and privately, knowing uninterrupted satisfaction and joy down through the years until eventually the angels come and carry us home to be with the Lord. Even then we will face death calmly and with full assurance!

So growing up is quite a shock! Life is not like that, and it is not like that for anybody. If I have learned anything in my years as a pastor, it is just how much suffering and unhappiness ordinary, average people face. We have become very good at hiding our problems from one another. People shake our hands and ask, 'How are you?' but instead of telling them, we reply, 'Fine, how are you?' And we do not want a truthful answer any more than they do. Time and again I have heard people say, 'If only my life were like Sally's (or Joe's, or Bert's, or Alice's),' when, if they had known what I knew about Sally's difficulties (or Joe's, Bert's, or Alice's) they would have been profoundly grateful that their lives were not like that. Life is unfair.

And it seems particularly unfair for the godly. Anyone who thinks that life is going to be much easier because they are a Christian invariably suffers a rude awakening. Christians experience all the difficulties of life that are common to everyone and in addition suffer the trials of being a Christian. 'All who desire to live godly in Christ Jesus will suffer persecution' (2 Timothy 3:12). Job is the supreme example of a godly man who suffered because he was godly. Why do these things happen?

If you have stayed with me this far hoping that eventually I will tell you the answer to that question, then I am afraid I must now disappoint you. Life **is** like that, and the Bible shows life is like that, but it does not tell us anywhere **why** life is like that. Even in this book of Job, we are given no complete explanation. But that does not mean that the Bible sheds **no** light at all on the problem; it does. What we must do now is explore what is often a forgotten factor in this whole matter of suffering. By looking partly at Job chapter twenty-one and also at a verse in Psalm 73 we will try to explain at least some of the mystery.

Spelling out the reality

Both this chapter and Psalm 73 insist again that the answer is not to be found in a simplistic and simple equation: the righteous prosper and the unrighteous suffer. Let us follow Job in this chapter as he spells out the reality.

Firstly, wicked men may live long and prosper. Look at verse 7 of Job 21: 'Why do wicked men live and become old, yes, become mighty in power?' Often, this happens not just when they ignore God, but when they actually curse him and deliberately turn their backs on him, saying, 'Depart from us, for we do not desire the knowledge of your ways. Who is the Almighty, that we should serve him?' (14,15). This is quite the opposite of what his friends are saying. They have admitted that the wicked man might possibly flourish for a little while, but shortly he will inevitably be cut down. No, says Job, that is not true; often they grow old and increase in power.

Secondly, Job points out that the wicked man may enjoy a good and rewarding family life. 'Their descendants are established with them in their sight and their offspring before their eyes' (verse 8). We feel Job's pain here; he is a righteous man, but he has lost his family.

Thirdly, he says that their homes are secure places. 'Their houses are safe from fear, neither is the rod of God upon them' (verse 9). Even their cattle will prosper (verse 10); again, remember that Job's livestock has been stolen or killed. Verses 11 and 12 speak of the joyful musical evenings the wicked enjoy in their homes, surrounded by their families, while righteous Job wails in misery.

Finally, to add insult to injury, not only are their lives prosperous but even their death is peaceful, for 'they go down to the grave in a moment' (verse 13). Sometimes we know that the wicked die in terror: Voltaire was one such. He dedicated his life to the destruction of Christianity, said of Christ, 'Curse the wretch!' and boasted 'In twenty years Christianity will be no more. My single hand shall destroy the edifice it took twelve apostles to rear.' But the physician who attended him at his death reported that he cried out desperately, 'I am abandoned by God and man! I will give you half of what I am worth if you will give me six months' life. Then I shall go to hell; and you will go with me. O Christ! O Jesus Christ!' and died in terror. But it is not always like that; it is not even usually like that. Casanova was so famous for his sexual immorality that even today his name is used as a nickname for an immoral man. But Casanova died in peace and is reported to have said on his death bed, 'I have lived as a philosopher and die as a Christian.' How easy it is to deceive ourselves! In fact, the wicked man may die in full vigour without ever having known debilitating illness (verse 23). Many regard that as a true blessing, and confess it to be an ambition; when their time 'to go' comes, they want to go quickly. But Job feels that his case is better described by verse 25—'another man dies in the bitterness of his soul never having eaten with pleasure.'

So Job spells out the reality, and calls his friends to face the facts. 'How often is the lamp of the wicked put out? How often does their destruction come upon them?' (verse 17). What about those who travel? Have you spoken to them? This is not only a local experience, it is universal. Have you paid no regard to their account? The evil man **is** spared from the day of calamity. He **is** delivered from the day of wrath.

Some have sought to solve the problem in a novel way, by arguing that a man may escape retribution for his sins, but his sons will suffer for it. Look at verse 19: 'They say, 'God lays up one's iniquity for his children." That was a common enough idea; there is even a proverb about it quoted in Scripture (though not with approval), 'The fathers have eaten sour grapes, and the children's teeth are set on edge' (Jeremiah 31:29). It is that same idea that Jesus is dealing with in John's gospel when asked the question about the man born blind.

Job complains quite rightly that this will not do as a solution. The idea is grossly unfair. If there is to be justice, let God's wrath come on the sinner himself; he must see and bear his own destruction. 'Let his eyes see his destruction, and let him drink the wrath of the Almighty; for what does he care about his household after him?' (verses 20,21).

Where the answer is to be found

It is this verse that points us to an answer. It is just a hint, but it is there. 'Let him drink the wrath of the Almighty.' It may seem that all men are the same in death, 'they lie down alike in the dust and worms cover them both' (verse 26) but that is not really the case. There is such a thing as the wrath of the Almighty, and there is more to life than this life.

In the last chapter we saw Job recall the great truth of the resurrection, and take his comfort and joy from that. In this chapter we must look briefly at the other side of that truth: the destiny of the wicked after death.

Psalm 73 also deals with the twin problems of the reality of suffering and the prosperity of the wicked. In many ways, that psalm is like a shorter version of the book of Job. It describes the prosperity of the wicked; they have no struggles, their bodies are healthy and strong, they are free from the burdens common to man, and so on. The author describes very honestly how he came to envy the arrogant, 'when I saw the prosperity of the wicked' (verse 3). This psalm too describes how the wicked mock God and refuse to recognise him: 'Is there knowledge in the Most High?' He agonises over this problem:

'When I thought how to understand this it was too painful for me...' (verse 16). But then he realised that he had not been facing all the facts: 'until I went into the sanctuary of God; then I understood their end' (17). However prosperous the wicked may be, and however much they may mock God, there is one fact that must not be forgotten: their final destiny. This much neglected fact now demands our attention.

Facing all the facts

Let us notice first that Christianity appeals to our **understanding**. When Karl Marx called religion the opiate of the people, he meant that it acts like a drug to dull the sense of pain that the masses feel. He believed that religion effectively kept the masses reasonably content and in their places by putting the fear of God into them. For him, religion was a great obstacle to the revolution that he believed was necessary. He knew that men would never be prepared to rebel against the instituted order while they believed that God had instituted that order. They would certainly never be prepared to rebel while they hoped for another world, or feared retribution in a world to come. Religion did not appeal to their understanding; it was the opiate of the people, designed to keep them asleep and to stop them thinking.

But according to the psalmist, true faith appeals to the understanding. The hope of a life to come is not an opiate; it is a matter of understanding: 'then I understood.' Dr. Lloyd-Jones comments: 'He did not merely feel better; he was put right in his thinking. He did not merely forget his problem for the time being; he found a solution... What happened to this man was not that he went to the Temple—into the church, so to speak—and that listening to the strains of beautiful music coming from the organ, and looking at the stained-glass windows and the beautiful lighting, he gradually began to feel a little bit better and forgot his troubles for the time being. No! It was something rational... it was a matter of understanding.' [1]

Contrast this with how many people escape the bare facts of life. What do they do? They go to their parties, get drunk and forget their problems for a while. Or they dance the night away until they are too tired to think and then drop into nothingness. It is not religion that is the opiate of the people; it is worldliness!

The gospel is different, and in the Bible the appeal is always made to the mind. That is why in evangelical churches so much prominence has traditionally been given to the sermon; it is appealing to the mind. When people are converted they need to be transformed by the renewing of their minds (Romans 12:2); the sermon is there because we need to be instructed and because our minds need to be furnished with truth. That is what Job needed. He had forgotten, briefly, that there is 'an end'—an ultimate destiny, an after-life. The psalmist had forgotten it too until he brought God into the picture. 'Until I went into the sanctuary of God...'

Christians are very foolish when they let their troubles or their low spiritual state keep them from church, but how often that happens. It is there, in the church with God's people met together and Jesus present with them, that we are likely to have our problems addressed and dealt with. When they **are** dealt with it is not by the general effect of the worship, but through our understanding. So often, our spiritual problems are caused by failing to understand, failing to reason things out, failing—in short—to bring God into the picture.

It is so important to take into account all the facts, visible as well as invisible. There is more to life than this life; though we are here for three score years and ten, God has put eternity into our hearts (Ecclesiastes 3:11). Every one of us has an immortal soul.

Final destiny

The father of Alexander the Great appointed a slave to remind him each morning of the fact of death; 'Philip, remember that you must die.' Death is described for us in the Bible like this: 'The dust will return to the earth as it was, and the spirit will return to God who gave it' (Ecclesiastes 12:7). So death breaks the cord that binds the spirit to the body; the body then begins to decay but the spirit does not. Instead, it returns to God. That explains the look of a dead body, as J. I. Packer rightly points out: 'It is sometimes said that the dead look peaceful, but this is hardly correct. What is true is that corpses look **vacant**. It is their evident emptiness that we find unnerving—the sense that the person whose body and face this was has simply **gone**.' [2] Note that, according to the Bible, this is true for both believers and unbelievers; in the story of the rich man and Lazarus, Jesus does not say Lazarus went to heaven ('Abraham's bosom') and the rich man ceased to exist. They are both described as going somewhere. It simply will not do to argue that because it is a parable we cannot take it too seriously. Parables are meant to teach lessons, and the lesson of this one is that both believer and unbeliever (good and wicked) continue to exist after their respective deaths, but in different places. After death, there are two destinies for the spirit. Every one of us goes to one or the other, and there is such a gulf fixed between the two (Luke 16:26) that no-one can ever cross. Those two destinies are heaven and hell and every man woman and child in the world at this moment will eventually find themselves in one or the other. There is no other alternative in Scripture; no 'purgatory' to get the not-quite perfect ready for heaven, and no neutral ground for those who are too good for hell but too bad for heaven.

What really matters then is our final destiny. A major problem in life is that people concentrate more on the road than on the final destination. The Lord Jesus spoke of two roads. One of them was broad and had a great deal of company on it. (In the days of our congested urban motorways that may not appeal to all of us! But the Lord is speaking of a very different situation; it was not a question of the road being congested but of there being safety in numbers.) The other road was a narrow one. On this road, the going is tough and every step along it is a hard-won victory. It is hardly surprising that there are not many on this road. Why should anyone travel such a route, when there is a quicker, clearer, wider, friendlier road to travel on? The only answer is this: they have different destinations. The broad road leads to destruction, and the narrow road leads to life. Those who are travelling on the narrow, hard, lonely, difficult road have recognised the importance of the destination. Choose the road according to where you want to go! Like so many of Jesus' illustrations, the point is an obvious one but the spiritual lessons are rarely followed.

What can we say about the final destiny that Jesus calls 'destruction'?

1. A place where inequalities are put right

It is of course hell that Jesus is describing by the word 'destruction', and according to the teaching of Jesus himself, hell is a place where all the inequalities of life are put right. In Matthew chapter 10, Jesus speaks to his disciples and says this about those who reject their words, 'Assuredly, I say to you, it will be more tolerable for the land of Sodom and Gomorrah in the day of judgement than for that city!' (verse 15). In Luke's Gospel he makes the same point as clearly as it could be made, 'That servant who knew his master's will, and did not prepare himself or do according to his will, shall be beaten with many stripes. But he who did not know, yet committed things worthy of stripes, shall be beaten with few. For everyone to whom much is given, from him much will be required...' (Luke 12:47,48).

Most of us would, I think, approve of this; plainly, not every sinner is a sinner of the same degree. At the same time we do need to remember, as evangelist John Blanchard puts it, 'Although not everyone will suffer to the same degree, none will suffer to a small degree. God's justice will ensure that the punishment fits the crime, but.. there are no 'little sins' because there is no little God to sin against. There will be no cool spots in hell.' [3]

It is increasingly common today to say that the traditional view of hell is wrong, and that the biblical language indicates that the unsaved are annihilated. They will point out, for example, that the Bible talks about the wicked being 'punished with everlasting destruction' (2 Thessalonians 1:9). When a thing is destroyed, they say, it ceases to be; so the destruction of the wicked means that they cease to exist, and there is no permanent suffering. There are several powerful objections to this though. For example, the language that is used in the Bible **never** means annihilated: 'the word rendered 'destruction' in 2 Thessalonians 1:9 (**olethros**) means, not annihilation, but ruin (cf. its use in 1 Thessalonians 5:3),' remarks Packer. [4] Then too, the pictures of hell in the Bible are inconsistent with annihilation. Jesus himself speaks of a devouring worm, unquenchable fire, outer darkness, a place of wailing and grinding of teeth. Some will be beaten with many stripes and some with few, says Jesus. It is because hell is a reality that for the first time in history all the inequalities will be put right. [5]

2. It is an eternal destiny

In one of the clearest passages of all the ones about judgement, Jesus said, 'These (the unsaved) will go away into everlasting punishment, but the righteous into eternal life' (Matthew 25:46). Actually, this is a very unfortunate translation, because the same Greek word (aionios) is translated first as everlasting and then as eternal, leaving room for the suspicion that there is some slight difference. But what the Lord clearly said is that the punishment of the wicked will last exactly as long as the life of the righteous. They are both eternal. Even more strikingly, exactly the same word is used of God himself in Romans 16:26, where he is described as 'the eternal God'. So, according to the Lord, the blessedness of heaven and the punishment of the wicked will both go on for as long as God exists; that is, for eternity. Any idea that the inhabitants of hell ever come to an end of their punishment is quite unscriptural.

This is not an easy truth but it will not do to dodge it just because we find it disturbing. If hell is real (and according to the Lord of heaven, who ought to know, it is) then we need to know it, and we need to avoid it. Those of us that know ourselves to be saved need to do far more to alert others of the danger they are in.

Our forefathers believed this doctrine, and it gave a power to their preaching which is all but unknown today. When Jonathan Edwards preached his famous sermon 'Sinners in the hands of an angry God' in the eighteenth century, it is said that such was the power of God on the preaching of that sermon that strong men took hold of the pillars of the church to stop themselves falling into hell. They held on so hard that their knuckles broke through the skin of their hands. Sadly, many today criticise Edwards for that sermon but we can be sure that those who took heed of his warning and fled to Christ as a result are everlastingly grateful for it!

3. A place of justice

The third thing we must say about hell is that it is a place of justice. The justice in hell is not softened with mercy at all, but nonetheless it is justice. Nobody in hell is ever punished more than he deserves. Again, I quote from John Blanchard, 'Because 'The Lord is righteous in all his ways,' (Psalm 145:17) he has never dealt unjustly with a single person in all of human history, and because 'he does not change like shifting shadows' (James 1:17) his impeccable justice will be revealed in all its glory on the final Day of Judgement. Millions of people (some, ironically, who had previously said they were atheists) have complained at God's dealings with them, but not a single complaint has ever been valid. The same will be true on the Day of Judgement.' [6]

To be told that those who are in hell are only getting exactly what they deserve is quite shocking! Yet we are fallen creatures, and our sense of right and wrong is twisted, perverted and fallible, like everything else about us. But God's sense of justice is none of these things; he is perfectly just to all those who are condemned for ever.

4. A place to be feared

We can readily see then that hell is not a place to be contemplated without fear! All the Biblical images of hell are images of terror. The most famous image of course is fire; fire which is ever burning but, like Moses' bush, never consuming. In that fire, said the Lord, is the undying worm, eating away (Mark 9:46).

Another terrifying image of hell is that of darkness—the outer darkness (Matthew 8:12, 22:13, 25:30). Do you know how terrifying darkness can be? Growing up in a town, surrounded always by well-lit houses and street lights, and never completely in the dark even during power cuts, I had never really understood this image. Then one day I happened to be travelling from my home in Aylesbury into London by train. I noticed that, unusually, there were no lights on the train we were travelling on. There are some tunnels on that line, but most of them are very short; we were no sooner in them, than out again. But there is one long tunnel on that line, just before the train enters Marylebone Station in London. As we pulled into that tunnel, the train began to slow down. As we reached the middle, it stopped! For some reason, there were no lights of any kind in that tunnel either; and the whole carriage was in real darkness. There was no glimmer of light anywhere. I had never been in such total darkness. I remember lifting my hand in front of my face and moving it around; I could not see anything at all. I am not given to panic, but I confess I did not say a word during all the time the train was stopped! How long had we stopped for? I had no way of knowing. I could not check my watch to see and I could not make any judgement about the passing of time from things I could see moving. I had heard stories of people cracking up in absolute darkness; now I believe it. When the Lord Jesus speaks of the outer darkness, it is an image of terror. God gives us these images in Scripture so that, knowing their truth, we may flee from that terror.

5. A place to which no-one need go

That leads me to the fifth thing I want to say about hell. It is a place to which nobody need go. God is a God of love as well as justice; his love will not prevent him exercising his justice, but he has demonstrated his love by sending his Son Jesus to be a Saviour.

We have seen how aware Job is of his sin. We have also seen him express his confidence that in the end he will dwell as a pardoned and justified soul in the presence of his Redeemer for ever. That of course is what the gospel is all about. God gave his Son that none should perish but have everlasting life. There are some who live without God and without hope in the world, whose final destiny is the outer darkness. There is nothing ultimately more miserable than the life of the unbeliever. Whether they prosper or not in this life, beyond death they have nothing to look forward to. But, 'the path of the just is like the shining sun that shines ever brighter unto the perfect day,' (Proverbs 4:18). 'Observe the upright: for the future of that man is peace,' (Psalm 37:37). Remember how the apostle Paul, an upright, just and godly man, contemplates his own imminent death. 'For I am already being poured out as a drink offering and the time of my departure is at hand. I have fought the good fight, I have finished the race, I have kept the faith. Finally there is laid up for me the crown of righteousness which the Lord, the righteous Judge, will give to me on that Day, and not to me only but also to all who have loved his appearing,' (2 Timothy 4:6,7,8).

A final solution

If this life is really all that there is, then there is no solution at all to the inequality and unfairness of life. But if, as the Bible consistently teaches, there is another life to come, then we can at least begin to feel our way forward towards a solution. Job's sufferings were so great that he expected to die. In those sufferings, he reached out to the certain hope of a life beyond death.

This is always where the Bible urges us to pin our faith. There may be great trials and difficulties for us in this life, but a Day of Judgement is coming. The wicked will perish, but for the righteous, 'the sufferings of this present time are not worthy to be compared with the glory which shall be revealed in us' (Romans 8:18). This is the other half of the argument; if the wicked prosper now, they will certainly be punished later. If the godly suffer now, they will certainly experience glory later. For all those who serve God truly, whatever their background, there is 'glory, honour and peace' (Romans 2:10). 'Eye has not seen, nor ear heard, nor have entered into the heart of man the things which God has prepared for those who love him. But God has revealed them to us through his Spirit' (1 Corinthians 2:9,10).

Chapter 8. Notes

1   **D.M. Lloyd Jones,** *Faith on Trial.* IVP.
2   **J.I. Packer,** *God's Words.* IVP.
3   **John Blanchard,** *Whatever happened to Hell.* Evangelical Press.
4   **ibid.**
5   The reality of hell as a place of conscious eternal punishment is well demonstrated in **Blanchard,** *Whatever happened to Hell.* Evangelical Press.

No through Road

Please read Job chapters 32 - 37

When Harold Kushner lost his son, the depth of his grief drove him to challenge his faith. Though a rabbi, and therefore presumably familiar with the book of Job, he eventually took refuge in a belief that God **could not** have prevented his son's death, or the many other similar tragedies. 'I can worship a God who hates suffering but cannot eliminate it, more easily than I can worship a God who chooses to make children suffer and die,' he said. The book he wrote from his experience[1] became a best-seller; many people seem to find his answer acceptable. As we continue our studies in Job we need to look at some of the inadequate answers that are often given to the problem of suffering. We will not try to look at all of them, only at those that are reflected in the closing chapters of Job. In this chapter, we will simply survey three possible, but wrong, answers. In later chapters we will examine how Job made some of these mistakes himself and then turn to how God rebukes Job for his mistakes and his arrogance.

The problem of Elihu

In chapter 32, a new character suddenly appears on the pages of Job. Elihu has not been mentioned before and, though 2:11 specifically speaks of Job's **three** friends coming to visit him, Elihu makes it clear (32:6,7) that he has been present all along. He is never mentioned until he begins to speak. When he has finished speaking, he is not mentioned again. But it is not the presence of Elihu that is the biggest enigma; it is the role he plays.

The commentators are divided in their understanding of his role and the division between them could hardly be more radical. I have on my desk at the moment two well-known commentaries on Job. One of them regards Elihu as speaking the words of God, in fact preparing the way for God himself who begins to speak in chapter 38. The other regards Elihu as the very mouthpiece of Satan; there is not much common ground between these two views!

Part of the confusion arises about Elihu simply because God passes no judgement on him, as he does on the other friends. One commentator argues that this is because God agrees with Elihu's assessment and therefore has no need to criticise him, but the other says it is because God regards Elihu's words as beneath contempt. Again, there is not much common ground here.

Then too, Job himself makes no response to Elihu. Elihu's speech is the longest in the book, and there are several places where he invites a response. But Job does not respond. Again, my two commentators are divided on the reason for this. One believes that it has all been said before, and Job cannot be bothered to go around the merry-go-round one more time but the other thinks that Elihu has convinced Job of his sin, and he is therefore speechless.

How are we to understand Elihu's role? Perhaps, in the absence of any other indication, we are wise to see what Elihu himself thinks he is doing, and take that at face value. In verse 2 and 3 of chapter 32, we see that Elihu is angry. First, he is angry with Job for justifying himself rather than God (verse 2), then he is angry with the friends because they have been unable to refute Job. So Elihu does not think Job is blameless, but he is not convinced either by the friends' assessment of Job's sin and character.

Not only is Elihu angry, he is also somewhat arrogant. He is far too sure of himself, even though he protests his humility: 'I am young in years and you are very old; therefore I was afraid, and dared not declare my opinion to you' (32:6). It is always difficult to believe anyone who tells us how humble they are! While Elihu has shown the traditional Eastern deference to age, as soon as he begins to speak all that deference seems to have gone. But it may simply be his youth that is the problem; all too often, humility is a grace that only comes with age.

In this chapter we will follow Elihu's argument and in doing so explore some of the roads that are blocked to us. That is, we will discover some of the answers that are sometimes given to the problem of suffering which are **not** options for anyone who takes the Scriptures seriously.

The need for revelation

Elihu stresses the need for revelation: 'I said 'Age should speak, and multitude of years should teach wisdom.' But there is a Spirit in man, and the breath of the Almighty gives him understanding,' (verses 7,8). One thing at least has become clear to Elihu as he has listened to these men: age alone does not bring wisdom. Mere human reflection and conversation and experience cannot solve all mysteries and in particular they can tell us very little about God. While there are some things about God which are clear from creation and conscience (see Romans 1) there are still many mysteries. If we are to know the answers to the great problems of life we need revelation from God.

Revelation is necessary simply because of our humanity. We are small, finite creatures, infinitely less than God. We cannot fathom all mysteries (even **with** the latest computers!). There are many things that we cannot know unless we are told. But revelation is also necessary because of our sinfulness. By nature, we no longer see God as clearly as we should. We are blind to his greatness (although Psalm 8 reminds us that creation speaks clearly enough of it) and to his holiness (although Romans 1:18ff says that even there we are without excuse).

There are many things that we cannot know unless God tells us himself; the great claim the Bible makes for itself is explained by Brian Edwards: 'the book that we call the Bible is God's collected revelation... Since men always wrongly interpret God's general revelation [creation and providence], God has given something simple, clear, sufficient and, like all of his revelation, perfect and without error; he has given us the Bible.' [2] Or as the writer to the Hebrews puts it, 'God... at various times and in different ways spoke in time past to the fathers by the prophets, [and] has in these last days spoken to us by his Son' (Hebrews 1:1,2). God has spoken! It is for this reason that we sit **under** the Bible's authority rather than **over** it; in it, God has spoken.

Then, having pointed out to us the need to have revelation if there is to be any adequate understanding of life in general and suffering in particular, Elihu deals with three wrong answers to the problem. He spells these out in 37: 23,24. ('As for the Almighty, we cannot find him; he is excellent in power, in judgement and abundant justice; he does not oppress. Therefore men fear him; he shows no partiality to any who are wise of heart' (or, following the NIV at this point, 'does he not have regard for all the wise in heart?'). There are three answers in this verse: 'he is excellent in power', so we must not say that he does not have the power to do anything about suffering. 'He is excellent... in justice and great righteousness' so we must not say that he is unrighteous and unjust in allowing suffering and finally 'does he not have regard for all the wise in heart?'—we must not say that God allows suffering because he just does not care. We will not look at them in that order, but in the order in which they first come up in his speech.

1. We must not say 'God is unfair, unjust'

'It is so unfair!' is a cry we often hear; and what people often seem to mean by it is that God himself is unfair. Sometimes, those who suffer speak of God as if he has a malicious streak that delights in causing suffering and torments for the sake of tormenting. Job would not go that far! Yet he has come close to it, certainly closer than he should. He has begun to wonder and speculate whether God is tormenting him without any reason at all. Certainly, Job has said that God is unfair (see chapter 10, for example). So Elihu quotes him, in order to rebuke him: 'Surely you have spoken in my hearing, and I have heard the sound of your words, saying 'I am pure, without transgression; I am innocent, and there is no iniquity in me. Yet he finds occasions against me, he counts me as his enemy,"' (33:8-10).

We may easily sympathise with Job here. Many of us, however well we know the Scriptures, have found ourselves saying—or at least thinking—the same things. 'Surely I have cleansed my hands in vain.' Rightly, Elihu rebukes Job for that: 'Whatever the answer may be, Job, and whatever you have been suffering, you ought not to have gone down that way! God is never unfair, and no believer should ever take this road in search of a solution to his problems.'

Zophar had said earlier (11:6) that Job was actually suffering **less** than he deserved. Although we criticised him for his heartlessness, there is a sense in which he was right. In one of her books Joni Eareckson quotes a comment from her father. We can imagine how much he, too, had suffered. Seeing his own beautiful, lively, energetic daughter suffer in such a dreadful way must have been hard to bear. But he was a Christian and on one occasion he said something that can be summarised like this: 'We Christians believe that we all deserve hell; and then, when we get less than hell, we moan and say God is unfair.' That is a very wise and godly response to suffering.

It **is** an uncomfortable truth to face, but we do deserve hell and so did Job. He was the most upright man on the face of the earth; we have God's own testimony to that. But like the rest of us he was also a dirty, vile and helpless sinner. Like the rest of us, he deserved hell for ever and ever. Like the rest of us, when he got less than hell, it was only because of God's grace and mercy. It is almost the definition of mercy: that we get less suffering than we deserve.

Job was right in protesting that there was no direct connection between his suffering and his sin. But he was wrong to imply that he had not sinned and wrong to say that he did not deserve what he was suffering. The distinction is important! Job's error led him to charge God with unfairness.

To point out the error of this thinking even more, Elihu speaks of two advantages that suffering may have in our lives. First, God may chasten us through suffering (33:14-22). The chastening of God is a sure sign of his love, (Hebrews 12:6); suffering is a rod he uses well! Second, God needs to woo us all from the jaws of distress (36:16, NIV) in order to lead us 'to a spacious place free from restriction.' In other words, this suffering is a part of the ongoing shepherding work which God performs in a believer's life, ensuring that his children stay within the boundaries of grace. No true child of God ever loses his salvation; whenever the child is about to wander too far, God woos him back. He does not ensure by the wave of a wand that our feet never wander, but he ensures that when they do, his providence brings us back. Commenting on Psalm 23:6 ('Surely goodness and mercy shall follow me all the days of my life; and I will dwell in the house of the Lord forever') one old commentator compared 'goodness' and 'mercy' to sheepdogs; when the sheep begins to wander, out goes one of the dogs, circling around, snapping at the heels, bringing it back. Sometimes, implies Elihu, God does that to us through suffering. There is a gracious purpose to everything God does, even when we do not know what it is.

2. We must not say 'God does not care'

The second route we must never take in our difficulties is the one that says that God does not care. More than once in his speech, Elihu points to the reality of God's care; this is how he puts it in 36:15: 'He delivers the poor in their affliction, and opens their ears in oppression.' Like Job, many of us have been here, and it is a very lonely place—even though so many visit it at one time or another! We know that God's word says we are to cast all our care on him because he cares for us, but at times the burden of care is so great that we find it hard to believe that God does care. And such is the subtlety of our sinful thinking that we can even justify this theologically: God is so great and powerful that he made the universe; how ridiculous then to believe that he could possibly be interested in me! 'When I consider your heavens, the work of your fingers, the moon and the stars which you have ordained, what is man that you are mindful of him, and the son of man that you visit him?' (Psalm 8:3,4). Isaiah makes the same point: 'Have you not known? Have you not heard? Has it not been told you from the beginning? Have you not understood from the foundations of the earth? It is he who sits above the circle of the earth, and its inhabitants are like grasshoppers' (Isaiah 40:21,22). But two things, at least, should persuade us of God's love.

a) The experience of discipline

As we have seen, Elihu implies that suffering can be God's chastening, to demonstrate his care and lead us back to righteousness: 'If they are bound in fetters, held in the cords of affliction, then he tells them their work and their transgressions... he also opens their ear to instruction... if they obey and serve him, they shall spend their days in prosperity and their years in pleasures,' (36:8,9,10,11). This theme is taken up by the writer to the Hebrews, who makes the point that God's chastening is a sign that we are his children; it demonstrates his love. In fact, he says, if we were not disciplined then it would prove that we were not God's children: 'My son, do not despise the chastening of the Lord... for whom the Lord loves he chastens, and scourges every son whom he receives... but if you are without chastening, of which all have become partakers, then you are illegitimate and not sons,' (Hebrews 12:5,6,8).

There is a story of a Christian man in the earlier part of this century who was the head of an orphanage. He tried hard always to treat the orphans as if they were his own children, and so was devastated one day when one of his former charges said to him, 'Of course we always knew which were your children and which were not; you treated us differently.' 'Oh,' said the man, 'In what way?' The reply came: 'You smacked your own children, but you never smacked us.' God's discipline may be painful but it is a proof that we are his children; his discipline proves his love. But there is a greater way in which God has proved his love.

b) The fact of the cross

One of the most influential theologians of this century was once asked what his greatest discovery was. Hesitating only a moment, the theologian replied with the words of the children's chorus: 'Jesus loves me this I know, for the Bible tells me so.' Marvellous discovery! But real love must be shown, not merely declared. What has God done to show that he loves us? 'God so loved the world that he gave his only begotten Son...'

We have already seen that there is only one anchor that can truly help us in times of major distress, only one thing that can still prove that God loves us when everything that happens to us seems to suggest otherwise. The state of the world cannot prove it, nor can our present happiness. But surely no Christian can ever sit under the shadow of the cross, and see the bleeding, agonising Saviour die, and still say, 'I just do not believe that God cares about me at all.' The more clearly we understand that cross, the firmer our faith must be. Let us then explore the doctrine of the cross a little more deeply by opening up one of the most important texts on the theme. In Galatians 2:20 Paul writes, 'The Son of God, who loved me, and gave himself for me.' To understand this text, let us consider it in three parts:

First, who he was. '**The Son of God** loved me...' says Paul. Who, precisely, is Jesus of Nazareth? What does the Bible say about him? The answer is profound: he is God appearing in the flesh, (1 Timothy 3:16). Sadly, we are so familiar with that truth (which is good) that it does not take our breath away as it should (which is bad). We believe that God himself came to the world in the person of Jesus. Though the Word was God (John 1:1), yet the Word became flesh and dwelt among us (John 1:14). Again and again in his Gospel John makes this great claim about Jesus: he is God. We do not do justice to the Biblical material unless we realise that the Lord Jesus Christ, who walked the earth as a man, and grew hungry and thirsty and tired and angry, was and is no less than God himself.

Second, what he did. 'He loved me, and **gave himself for me...**' Scripture says, 'Let us not love in word or in tongue, but in deed and in truth,' (1 John 3:18) and it is God himself who has given us the supreme example of such a love. If God had loved the world, but done nothing, how different things would be! But here Paul reminds us that real love has acted; and Jesus gave himself.

The full extent of that giving can be seen clearly in Philippians 2, where Paul outlines at least three stages in this self-giving of the Lord Jesus. God became a man, that man died, and his death was a curse.

God became a man. Although he was in the form of God, equal with God in every way, he did not count that equality with God as something to be used for his own advantage (which is what the Greek word **harpagmos** literally means) but, for the sake of others, he became a man. No number of illustrations can adequately describe this humbling! If we talk of a man becoming a slug, or an ant, or a microbe to try and illustrate this, every illustration must fail. Men, slugs, ants and microbes are all part of creation but the Son of God is the Creator himself, and crossed the great divide for our sake.

That man died. 'He humbled himself and became obedient to death...' (verse 8). The NKJV is misleading at this point to insert the extra words 'the point of' here (he humbled himself and became obedient *to the point of* death) as if implying that he stopped short of actually dying. He humbled himself and became obedient even to the point of surrendering his life. There is surely no greater mystery in the Bible than this mystery: the immortal bows to mortality, the prince of life submits to death, the eternal dies.

That death was a curse. 'Even the death of the cross,' says Paul, and he does not simply have in mind the great torture and pain that the victim of crucifixion must endure. God's law declares 'Cursed is everyone who hangs on a tree,' (Galatians 3:13, see Deuteronomy 21:23) and when Jesus died he was voluntarily submitting to the curse of God. He who, from the beginning, was 'face to face with God' (which is what John 1:1 says in a literal translation) now endured God turning his face away. When Christ cried out 'My God, my God, why have you forsaken me?' (Mark 15:34), he was enduring the curse and, in a very real sense, tasting hell itself. So, when Paul writes 'he loved me and gave himself for me,' he has all this in mind and more.

Third, who he did it for. 'He loved **me** and gave himself for **me**.' It is an amazing thing that Christ should love the world; it is a more amazing thing that he should love me. Paul's passionate evangelism to both Jew and Gentile over many years demonstrates clearly his own conviction that Jesus was the Saviour of the world. Here though he expresses his conviction that the death of Jesus was a very particular thing. To use the theological terms, the atonement is a particular atonement, an atonement aimed at specific people. There is nothing 'hit and miss' about the cross of Jesus; it is no desperate attempt by an impotent God to save somebody, anybody. Jesus said, 'I lay down my life for the sheep,' (John 10:15).

This is an important truth. For whom did Jesus die? Perhaps you have never realised just how contentious a question that is among Christians! But let us try to avoid the contention by asking what the question means. If it means, 'Who may be saved by the death of Jesus?' then surely there is no argument. Anybody who wishes to be saved, may be saved. 'Whoever desires, let him take the water of life freely,' (Revelation 22:17). God 'commands all men everywhere to repent,' (Acts 17:30). But if we ask what God was trying to achieve by the death of Jesus, then the answer is inevitably different. Was he trying to save everybody? For if so, he has failed; not everybody is saved and hell is not empty. Does the Bible present God as one who fails at all? Of course not!

John Owen's classic book **The Death of Death in the Death of Christ** famously summarises the situation like this. There are only two alternatives: one is that there is something lacking in the death of Christ that we must make up by ourselves; those who succeed in making up this deficiency go to heaven, those who fail go to hell. If that is the case, then those in heaven have something to boast about—which is contrary to Scripture (Romans 4:2, for example). The other alternative is described by Roy Clements: 'If that is not right, we can come to only one other conclusion: Namely, that in the intention and purpose of God, when he thought this all out before the foundation of the world, Jesus' death on the cross was a substitutionary sacrifice not for everybody, but for a particular company, those whom the bible often calls his chosen or 'elect." [3]

It is in this way, as a death aimed at saving a definite people, that the Bible consistently presents the death of Jesus. And for our purpose this is important for one vital reason: when we suffer, and come to the cross for our comfort, we are seeing a love which is specific, aimed at those God chose before the foundation of the world (Ephesians 1:4). And this love has succeeded in its purpose. As Spurgeon put it more than a century ago, 'We say Christ so died that he infallibly secured the salvation of a multitude that no man can number, who through Christ's death not only may be saved, but are saved, must be saved and cannot by any possibility run the hazard of being anything but saved.'

What has this to do with our suffering? Everything! For when we come to the cross for comfort, and are assured by it that God has loved us, we are being assured that he loved us **specifically and individually.** Even our sufferings therefore must be a manifestation of that love. When we really grasp this we cannot begin to doubt his love or his care. We go from the darkness of despair to the blazing light of Calvary.

3. We must not say 'God does not have the power to do anything about our situation.'

The third 'forbidden' way out of the problem of suffering is the one taken by Harold Kushner, described at the beginning of this chapter. It is to argue that God is not really sovereign; he does not have the power to prevent suffering. Although this seems attractive, and even inevitable to some, it would leave us with a God who is simply not God at all.

Elihu deals this view a death blow; he spends almost a chapter and a half dealing with it: 'God is exalted by his power,' (36:22) he says. We need to let God be God!

In our first chapter we looked at the biblical teaching that God is in control of all things. He works all things according to the counsel of his will (Ephesians 1:11). Everything, without any exception at all, is under his sovereign control. When a sparrow falls from heaven, it is God who is in control—Jesus said so. There are no limits to the power of God; the only limits on God are moral limits; he cannot sin, he cannot lie, he cannot deny himself (Hebrews. 6:18, 2 Timothy 2:13). We need to understand just how great and powerful God is, and let God be God.

How great is God? David Watson tells the following story to show just how small we are and therefore, conversely, how great God is: 'Franklin Roosevelt used to have a little ritual with the famous naturalist William Beebe. After an evening's chat the two men would go outside and look into the night sky. Gazing into the stars they would find the lower left-hand corner of the great square of Pegasus. One of them would recite these words as part of their ritual: 'That is the spiral galaxy of Andromeda. It is as large as our Milky Way. It is one of a hundred million galaxies. It is 750000 light years away. It consists of one hundred billion suns, each larger than our own sun.' They would then pause, and Roosevelt would finally say, 'Now I think we feel small enough. Let's go to bed.' " [4] They could just as easily have said, 'Now we are beginning to understand how great God is,' for God is the one who brought all this into being—just by speaking! ('God said, Let there be... and there was...', Genesis 1:3,6,14) 'How great is God—beyond our understanding!' (36:26).

Elihu's way of emphasising God's greatness is not so very different from Roosevelt's, for Roosevelt looked at the universe and Elihu looks at the weather. He describes the rain (36:27), the thunder (29) and the lightning (38:35). He describes the storm (37:3-5) and the snow (6). He speaks of the freezing of the waters (10) and the brightness of the sun (21). 'Now Job,' he seems to say; 'answer me. How can anyone think God's power is limited? Whatever the answer to your sufferings may be, this is not it!'

Job and his friends were alike in one way; they were not prepared to let God be God. They were not prepared for there to be a mystery in God's dealings. They wanted to know, even as God knew. But that desire to be like God in knowledge was the original sin; Eve was tempted to eat the fruit of the tree of knowledge with the promise that she would be like God, knowing good and evil. Sadly, through the long centuries, very little has changed. We still want to know and we rebel against ignorance.

Rebelling against ignorance is just what Kushner is doing. Understandable though it may be in his circumstances, his solution actually creates more problems than it solves. It not only gives us a God who is not God, it has two other effects which are pointed out by Don Carson. First, it leaves us unsure how the world will turn out. The Bible paints a picture of God's ultimate victory, and it does so on the basis of a God who is all-powerful. But if he is not all-powerful at all, then the odds are no better than even that evil will not, in the end, triumph. The second problem is that it leaves us with a God who cannot help, and the cost is just too great. There is no point in asking Kushner's God for help because 'He is already doing the best he can, poor chap... For all that one sympathises with Kushner's search for a God he can respect, he has ended up with a god who cannot help.' [5]

Sometimes, with God, we have to accept that there are things we cannot know. There is an answer to the problems of the world, but he has not chosen to tell us what it is. The secret things still belong to the Lord our God. Often, we have to be content merely to know what the answers are not; faith is trusting God when we cannot see. We walk by faith, not by sight, (2 Corinthians 5:7).

Chapter 9 Notes

1   **Harold Kushner,** *When bad things happen to good people.* Schocken.
2   **Brian Edwards,** *Nothing But the Truth,* Evangelical Press.
3   **Roy Clements,** *Rescue: God's Promise to Save.* Christian Focus.
4   **David Watson,** *In search of God.* Falcon.
5   **Don Carson,** *How Long, O Lord?* IVP.

The impatience of Job

Please read Job chapter 23

Martin Luther was on trial for his life. Called by the church authorities to recant his teaching, and aware that his life was at risk, he asked for time to think, pray and meditate. The authorities gave him twenty-four hours. That night, Luther prayed. He had rediscovered the gospel that the church had tried (with considerable success) to hide. He had begun to make it known and the great Reformation was under way. Soon it would sweep across Europe, bringing gospel light to thousands who walked in darkness and altering the destinies of nations for centuries and individuals for eternity. It could not possibly have been more important for Luther to stand firm. Alone and friendless in his cell, he called on the God he served—and got no answer. His spirit was cold, the heavens seemed as brass against him, and in despair he wrote 'O my God, where art thou? The devils rage, and thou art not there. The devils hound me, but where art thou? O my God, art thou dead?' [1] The prophet Isaiah had said, 'Truly, you are God, who hide yourself, O God of Israel, the Saviour,' (45:15) and that was certainly Luther's own painful experience.

Job's experience was similar. 'You have heard of the patience of Job,' says the Authorised Version of James 5:11, and it has become proverbial: 'He must have the patience of Job!' Actually, this is a poor translation of the verse, which is much better rendered in the NKJV: 'You have heard of the **perseverance** of Job.' John Blanchard, commenting on the fact that James uses the word **hupomone** (perseverance) not **makrothumia** (patience), remarks: 'The difference lies in the fact that hupomone is not so much a matter of patience with people (Job did not in fact excel in that department) but rather a steadfast endurance of adverse circumstances.' [2] Job did in fact persevere to the end, though from our perspective it seems, at times, to have been a near thing. But he was not always patient, either with other people or even with God himself. Now, in chapter 23, Job laments that he has lost touch with God: 'Oh, that I knew where I might find him...' (verse 3). To all his other problems is added this one: his experience of communion with God is broken. He tells us how hard he has tried to restore that communion: 'Look, I go forward, but he is not there, and backward, but I cannot perceive him; when he works on the left hand I cannot behold him; when he turns to the right hand, I cannot see him,' (23:8,9). Job has not become spiritually lazy; he is actively doing what he can to restore his sense of communion with God, but he is failing. 'The Lord is good, a stronghold in the day of trouble,' says Nahum (1:7). Job's head may well say 'Amen' to that, but his heart is another matter!

Spiritual desertion

Occasionally, I meet with people who have been Christians a long time who tell me that they have never known any sense of being deserted by God. When they read these words of Job, (or words like those of Luther) they can barely understand them. I have come to believe that these people have a very poor experience of spiritual communion. They have not really known great depths in their spiritual lives and their knowledge of God is very shallow; what they have never had, they cannot lose! But Job is in very good company: Jesus himself experienced spiritual desertion and cried out from the cross, 'My God, my God why have you forsaken me?' (Matthew 27:46). Jesus' experience has a unique quality to it, but many saints down the ages have experienced similar things. The stories of men like Jim Elliot or Hudson Taylor, George Whitefield or John Wesley show just how shallow most Christian experience is today. But these men knew too what it was to have times when they were close to despair, times when they looked for light but found darkness (see Isaiah 59:9), times when they could certainly have cried out with Job, 'Oh, that I knew where I might find him!'

There are many such experiences recorded in Scripture. Several of the psalms have been described as 'songs of the night' precisely because they relate this kind of experience. Psalm 74, for example, deals with the problem of God's apparent absence from the church. 'O God, why have you cast us off forever?' it begins, leading to 'Arise, O God, plead your own cause' (verse 22), after the psalmist has listed the evidence that leads him to believe that God has withdrawn from them. But it is Psalm 77 which comes nearest to describing Job's own experience: I cried out to God with my voice... in the day of my trouble I sought the Lord; my hand was stretched out in the night without ceasing; my soul refused to be comforted... Has his mercy ceased forever? Has his promise failed for evermore? Has God forgotten to be gracious?' (verses 1,2, 8-9). This psalmist has a problem which is very much like Job's, and he tells us what he has done about it. He has reminded himself of the history of his people, the 'years of the right hand of the Most High' (verse 10)—that is, the times when God has **proved** his grace and compassion. He has taken hold of himself, refusing to give in to despair; and yet it seems to make very little difference. Suddenly, in the midst of remembering God's miracles through Moses, the psalm just stops! There is no note of triumph to end on. There is no renewed confidence in God's mercy, in spite of the fact that the psalmist has undoubtedly done the right things. Why does the psalm stop like this? Surely it is because even doing 'the right things' is not helping him at this time; his despair is still great and he still seems to be out of touch with the living God. In this, he is just like Job. 'Oh that I knew where I might find him.'

Job has not got his theology wrong here. God is omnipresent, and Job has not forgotten that. There is nowhere in all creation that lacks the presence of God: 'If I ascend into heaven, you are there; if I make my bed in hell, behold, you are there. If I take the wings of the morning, and dwell in the uttermost parts of the sea, even there your hand shall lead me, and your right hand shall lead me' (Psalm 139:8-10). Job is only describing his own feelings here, not the objective facts; at this moment, his experience is that of having been deserted by God.

The preservation of the saints

Job has not lost his salvation; no child of God ever can. One of the most comforting truths that we all need to hold on to during times of trial is this one, and it is a truth we can be sure of for at least two reasons.

Specific scriptures

First, we may be sure of this because of the many specific Scriptures which teach it. One of the clearest of these comes from the mouth of the Lord Jesus himself, who said of his sheep, 'I give them eternal life, and they shall never perish, neither shall anyone snatch them out of my hand. My Father, who has given them to me, is greater than all, and no one is able to snatch them out of my Father's hand' (John 10:28,29). There is no one in the whole universe strong enough to steal Jesus' sheep from him. Such is the power of Jesus that those who are once saved by him are undoubtedly kept to the very end. Yet, as if that were not enough, Jesus promises that believers are held in the Father's hand too; a double omnipotence prevents the loss of a single sheep.

I remember an old and godly man commenting on this passage rather like this: 'It says, 'No-one can snatch them out of my hand.' But it does not say that they can never leave his hand if they choose to.' There are many things that could be said in answer to this, but the chief is that it misses the clear statement of the Lord himself. 'I give them eternal life,' he said, '**and they shall never perish.**' It could hardly be any clearer than that! Peter makes much the same point when he writes of the eternal inheritance kept in heaven for believers 'who are kept by the power of God through faith for salvation ready to be revealed in the last time,' (1 Peter 1:5). And Paul chimes in too, declaring 'There is therefore now no condemnation to those who are in Christ Jesus... For I am persuaded that neither death nor life, nor angels nor principalities nor powers, nor things present nor things to come, nor height nor depth, nor any other created thing, shall be able to separate us from the love of God which is in Christ Jesus our Lord,' (Romans 8:1, 38-39).

The nature of salvation

Second, we may be sure of this truth because the nature of salvation demands it. Salvation is the giving of everlasting life, and 'he who believes in the Son has everlasting life' (John 3:36). It is difficult to understand how anybody can have **everlasting** life—temporarily! The Bible's teaching on justification leads to the same inevitable conclusion. What is justification? It is the verdict of a law court, by which the accused is declared to be innocent before the law and therefore free to go. Believers are justified by faith in Christ, and their justification is the judgement of the last day brought forward into time. It is not possible to be justified **now** from our sins and condemned **tomorrow** or else justification was never real in the first place. God's verdict, once pronounced, can never be changed. As we saw from Romans 8 a little earlier, 'There is therefore now no condemnation to those who are in Christ Jesus.'

This is a great truth! It is also a very practical truth, with the power to save us from spiritual despair when 'all around my soul gives way.' But though a believer will never lose his salvation, he may certainly lose the enjoyment of his salvation for a while. After his sin with Bathsheba, David prayed 'Restore to me the joy of your salvation' (Psalm 51:12). His sin caused him to lose his sense of communion with God; Job had lost that too. The question I want to try and explore in this chapter is, why? What happens to cause us to lose that sense of God's presence? Is it always sin that does it, is it always our own fault? Or may there be other reasons?

1. Sin

Sin certainly can break our enjoyment of fellowship with God, as we saw from David's prayer, 'Restore to me the joy of your salvation.' God is light, and light can have no fellowship with darkness. 'Do not grieve the Holy Spirit of God, by whom you were sealed for the day of redemption,' says Paul (Ephesians 4:30). It is possible to grieve him, and so lose the comfort of his presence. He will not, generally speaking, come and whisper his mercies to us when we are determined to continue in sin. He will not comfort and console us in times of distress if we are clinging to something that we know grieves him. 'If I regard iniquity in my heart, the Lord will not hear' (Psalm 66:18). We must never underestimate the effect of sin in the life of the Christian. It can and does spoil our enjoyment of God.

But is sin **always** the explanation? What about the Lord Jesus on the cross, when he cried out 'My God, my God, why have you forsaken me?' (Matthew 27:46). Plainly, Jesus felt that his own communion with the Father had been broken. Was sin at the root of this too? Yes, it was; but not his own sin, for Jesus, though tempted in every way as we are, was without sin (see Hebrews 4:15). But on the cross the Lord laid on him our iniquity; though he knew no sin, God made him to be sin for us (see Isaiah 53:6, 2 Corinthians 5:21). When he became sin, the pure and holy Father turned away. Even here, sin was the root cause.

When a Christian's communion with God is damaged, it is **often** sin at the root. Yet not always, as we will see.

2. Exhaustion

After Elijah had the famous victory on Mount Carmel, and God vindicated him before all the people, the very next thing that happens is that Elijah runs away (1 Kings 19:3)! The great prophet suddenly becomes afraid of one woman, and it is not long before he is crying out to die. 'It is enough! Now, Lord, take my life, for I am no better than my fathers!' (1 Kings 19:4). It may be that this desolation too is accounted for at least partly by sin; running from Jezebel as he did was hardly faith. But it seems clear from the way that God dealt with him that Elijah had a much more basic problem. He was exhausted. After he has prayed to die, he lies down and sleeps until an angel wakes him, feeds him, and tells him to sleep again. Then the whole cycle is repeated before Elijah is ready to face God's challenge about his running away, 'What are you doing here, Elijah?' God who knows our frame and remembers that we are only dust (Psalm 103:14), recognised that Elijah's primary problem was physical, not spiritual. It has been my own experience on many occasions as a pastor that when people come to me to say how far from God they feel, a little probing reveals that they are just doing far too much and are at the end of their resources. The last thing such people need is to be told to discipline themselves more. They do not need longer devotional times, but longer sleep times. They do not need to get more involved in the work of the church, they need to take a holiday. If we do not pace ourselves and eat, sleep and exercise properly, we can become so exhausted that we lose all sense of enjoyment of God.

3. Illness and pain

The great evangelist George Whitefield once lamented his lack of the sense of God's presence. At first, he tells us, he thought sin had driven him away, but then he realised it was only toothache! This is similar to the problem of exhaustion; the state of our bodies can have a spiritual impact on us.

So in times when we do not seem to feel much of God's presence, we do need to ask ourselves honestly if sin is coming between us. But that does not mean unrealistic and destructive self-examination; it is hard to sin without knowing it. When David lost his sense of God's presence, he knew what he had done with Bathsheba. He simply needed to face up to it. Then, if as far as we can see there is no spiritual problem, and if we have prayed 'Cleanse me from secret faults' (Psalm 19:12), we need to look for other explanations.

It may not always be straightforward. Elijah was exhausted but had fled from Jezebel and both things needed to be dealt with in their proper order. So, undoubtedly, it was with Job. Can we doubt that his bereavement and his illness (and his friends!) had done much to contribute toward this sense of God's missing presence? But there were, as Elihu points out, spiritual (that is, sinful) seeds to this fruit as well. Job's **sufferings** were not in any way caused by his sin; but his sense of spiritual desolation was. Let us look at some of the sins that Elihu highlights.

1. Calling God unrighteous

Elihu highlights this in 33:8-10. 'I have heard the sound of your words, saying 'I am pure, without transgression; I am innocent, and there is no iniquity in me. Yet he finds occasions against me, he counts me as his enemy.' Job has argued that God is unrighteous and Elihu responds to this in 34:10, 'Far be it from God to do wickedness,' and goes on 'It is unthinkable that God would do wrong, that the Almighty would pervert justice' (34:12, NIV). It is unthinkable and Job ought never to have thought it. When the thought occurred to him, he ought to have dismissed it immediately; as one old saint is reported to have said, 'You may not be able to stop birds flying above your head but you can stop them nesting in your hair!'

Elihu applies a marvellous logic to Job's position here. 'If he should set his heart on it, if he should gather to himself his Spirit and his breath, all flesh would perish together and man would return to dust' (34:14,15). That is, if God wanted to crush you (or anybody) he would have done a better job of it than this! Then he goes on, 'Should one who hates justice govern?' That is, how could God govern if he were unjust? If God were as unjust as Job has implied there would be no justice in the universe. Job has said the unthinkable, and the Spirit is grieved.

2. Thinking like the worldling

Job has also been guilty of worldly or unspiritual thinking. He had said, 'It profits a man nothing that he should delight in God,' and 'What profit shall I have more than if I had sinned?' (34:9, 35:3).

Sadly, inside and outside the churches many people think like this. 'The fool has said in his heart, 'There is no God" (Psalm 14:1). A man who behaves wickedly (for 'fool' in the Hebrew has that meaning) is behaving as if there is no God to reward right and wrong. Some who claim to be believers fall into the same trap, arguing that because God forgives sin, it does not matter whether we sin or not. We may abound in sin, that grace may abound even more (see Romans 6:1). But the sins of believers can have profound effects. Moses merely struck a rock, and God forbade him from entering the Promised Land as a punishment. Ananias and Sapphira 'only' told a lie, and were immediately struck dead. And David, who fled from Saul into the company of the ungodly, caused the death of a whole city (see 1 Samuel 22:22). Sin **never** turns out to be the easy option.

3. Refusing to repent

This is brought out helpfully in the NIV translation of Elihu's words. 'Suppose a man says to God, 'I am guilty but will offend no more. ... Should God then reward you on your terms, when you refuse to repent?' (34:31,33). In many ways, Job has gone too far. He has allowed thoughts to take root that he should have dismissed at once and he has uttered words that ought never to have passed his lips. Elihu acknowledges that such things happen and we know it too. 'If anyone does not stumble in word, he is a perfect man, able also to bridle the whole body' (James 3:2). Once these things had been pointed out to Job the proper response was one of repentance, but Job continues to justify himself. He finds it easier to carry on, rather than to turn back. How common a problem this is, even in human relationships. So many marital arguments, for example, are caused by one partner or the other (and often both) refusing to acknowledge their wrong and to repent of it. Instead of backtracking the partners simply keep pushing, but the only way to restore marital harmony is to go back and repent. Many marriages eventually explode apart just because such sins are never dealt with. If this is important in human relationships, it is much more so in our walk with God. Job could not go forward until he went back; there was no way ahead for him until he repented.

4. Forgetting the greatness of God

Job had simply forgotten how great God is, and how far removed from the littleness of man he is. Elihu reminds him of this in 36:22-26. Job had wanted God to behave and do just like a man would behave and do; but God is greater than man. 'My thoughts are not your thoughts, nor are your ways my ways, says the Lord' (Isaiah 55:8). So Elihu reminds Job of the foolishness of pitting himself against the Almighty: 'Stand still and consider the wondrous works of God' (37:14). It is a theme which God himself takes up before the book ends.

So: what could Job have done to avoid damaging his sense of fellowship with God? What must **we** do in times of difficulty (when we most need to know the presence of the everlasting arms underneath us) if we are not to feel deserted by God?

First, avoid sin. It is so easy in times of difficulty to think, 'What difference could it possibly make now if I sinned? Things could not get any worse.' But they can always get worse and there is nothing worse than reaching a point where we feel forsaken by God.

Second, think in a spiritual manner. We have referred several times in these studies to Psalm 73, which begins 'Surely God is good to Israel.' That is where the psalm begins, but it is not where the psalmist had begun! It took him a while to shrug off worldly thinking, but when he remembered the goodness of God he took a stand on solid ground. It is so easy to fail here, and let our circumstances so dominate our thinking that we just travel round in circles. 'There is no avoiding the truth,' we may tell ourselves. 'I have tried to serve God and I am suffering so there is no point in serving God at all.' Spiritual thinking breaks that vicious circle of thought by taking a stand on a truth that God has revealed (in this case, on the goodness of God) and insisting on using that to interpret events. We must never let events interpret truth!

Third, face all the facts. Again, Psalm 73 is a help here. Faced with the horror of the ungodly prospering, he finds his spiritual balance thrown. Why? Because he is only facing some of the facts. Eventually, though, he faces them all; 'I went into the sanctuary of God; then I understood their end. Surely you set them in slippery places; you cast them down to destruction' (Psalm 73:17,18). Hell is a reality; the punishment of the ungodly is a fact we need always to take into account. Job, however, had forgotten this; the only facts he could see were the facts of his own suffering. Though from time to time he remembered better things (19:25, for example) yet the bulk of his speeches are uttered in a spirit of doubt and even unbelief. Most of us, of course, would fail even more than Job did, if we suffered as he had! But even so, he ought to have remembered all the facts. His suffering could only be for a moment, and eternity is a very long time. It would have put a different complexion on things altogether.

Fourth, we need to remember who we are. Job has set himself up against God. Although he earlier acknowledged that between them there could be 'no contest', yet in effect he has challenged God's rights and power. We do this so easily! Eventually, though, Job saw the error of this, and put his hand over his mouth (40:4). 'Be slow to speak,' says the Bible (James 1:19), and we must be particularly slow to speak against God. We must not act as if we knew everything and he was answerable to us. Job ought to have covered his mouth earlier—and his friends should have joined him! The Book of Proverbs says, 'Even a fool is counted wise when he holds his peace,' (Proverbs 17:28) and these men would have seemed much wiser if they had been content to remain silent. We have to be content not to comprehend fully what God is doing. Faith is being willing to trust when we cannot see.

Is it right then to speak of the patience of Job? No. Job persevered through his sufferings but patience was not his strong point. As a result, he lost contact with the God who would have sustained him, and thus made his sufferings all the more painful. We will be wise indeed if we can avoid this error!

Chapter 10. Notes

1   Quoted in **R.T. Kendall,** *Jonah.* Hodder and Stoughton.
2   **John Blanchard,** *Truth for Life.* Evangelical Press.

God's true purpose

Please read Philippians 2:5-11

Have you seen the car sticker that reads, 'Quick! Hire a teenager while they still know everything!'? A mother who was trying to cook was being pestered by her teen-age daughter who had just started cookery lessons at school. The girl could not refrain from commenting and criticising; everything her mother did was wrong. 'You shouldn't be doing that,' she said. 'That's not right. The oven isn't hot enough. It won't cook properly unless you have it much hotter than that. COCONUT!? You don't put coconut in Yorkshire puddings!' At this point, the patient mother turned to her daughter and said, 'No, dear. But I'm not making Yorkshire puddings!' Part of our problem with the things that happen in the world, especially suffering, is like that. We think we know what God is doing, and yet the events of the world, and of our lives, do not fit that anymore than coconut goes in a Yorkshire pudding. If God's aim is to make every individual as happy as possible on the earth, then suffering is truly inexplicable. But if God is not doing that at all, but something else, then there **may** be an explanation. It may well not be the explanation that we expect or want and it may be one that is totally incomprehensible to those who do not know Christ as Lord. But it may, nonetheless, be the truth.

Job's repeated mistake was that he misunderstood what God was doing. It was never part of God's plan to keep Job happy throughout life; that is not what the universe was built for.

Why was the universe ever made? The whole of creation was made to bring glory to God; everything in the universe was made for that purpose alone. Job's sufferings were used **by** God to bring glory **to** God. Satan had said, 'Job only serves you because it pays him,' and God had replied in effect, 'No; Job serves me because I am worth serving.' Satan challenged God to prove it and God did prove it. Job was the battle ground.

But it is the New Testament, not the Old, that gives us most insight into what God is doing in the world. The clearest explanation of all is in Philippians 2, where Paul tells us that it is the eternal purpose of God to exalt the Lord Jesus. At **his** name, every knee should bow. In this chapter we will turn away from Job for a while and examine what God says in that passage.

God made the universe for his own glory

'...at the name of Jesus, every knee should bow, of those in heaven, and of those on earth, and of those under the earth, and that every tongue should confess that Jesus Christ is Lord, **to the glory of God the Father**' (Philippians 2:10,11). This is a truth the Scripture makes very clear in numerous places. For example, Isaiah 43:7 teaches that God's sons and daughters (his own people both in the Old and New Testaments) are those 'whom I have created for my glory.' The universe itself, in all its variety and vastness, proclaims the glory of God to any who will listen: 'The heavens declare the glory of God, and the firmament shows his handiwork,' (Psalm 19:1). When the book of Revelation lifts the curtain on the worship in heaven itself, those before the throne declare that God is worthy of glory because he is Creator: 'You are worthy, O Lord, to receive glory and honour and power; for you created all things, and by your will they exist and were created,' (Revelation 4:11). And Paul's great doxology in Romans 11 concludes with the words, 'For of him and through him and to him are all things, to whom be glory forever, Amen' (Romans 11:36). The universe demonstrates the magnificent excellence of God by showing his wisdom and his power. The human race is part of that creation and in a unique position to bring glory to the Creator since we alone were made in the image (likeness) of God. More than anything else, God's purpose to save a vast multitude that no-one could number, and to do so at the cost of his only beloved Son, declares the glory of his love. Even hell itself declares the glory of his justice (Romans 9:22,23).

The glory of God is the chief thing in the world. This is not something that the unbeliever particularly finds easy to accept. Brian Edwards relates how he was challenged by his GP to explain how he could believe in a God who allowed so much suffering. He had five minutes of surgery time to do it and, he says, he inevitably failed. But he left the doctor with one challenge: 'You may not find my explanation satisfactory, but at least with a belief in God I do have an answer to give; with no belief in God you face the same problem without any answer.' [1] The doctor had the grace to concede the truth of that, and so must we.

God's ultimate purpose

God made the universe for his own glory. Actually we can say rather more than that from our passage in Philippians. It is the ultimate purpose of God the Father to bring glory to God the Son; God 'has highly exalted him and given him the name which is above every name, that at the name of Jesus every knee should bow, of those in heaven, and of those on earth, and of those under the earth, and that **every tongue should confess that Jesus Christ is Lord**, to the glory of God the Father. Why is this God's chosen purpose?

Firstly, it is because of the person of Jesus: that is, it is because of who he is. Jesus is no less than God himself, and because he **is** God, it is right that at his name every knee should bow. The 'name' of Jesus at which everyone will bow is undoubtedly Jehovah, for to confess that 'Jesus Christ is Lord' is to confess just that: Jesus Christ is Jehovah.

Secondly, it is because of the love of the Father for the Son. Between the Father and the Son there is an eternal relationship of love. Many times Jesus speaks of his Father's love for him: 'The Father loves the Son, and has given all things into his hand,' he says in John 3:35. Again, in John 5:20, Jesus says 'For the Father loves the Son and shows him all things that he himself does: and in John 15:9 the eternal character of that love is expressed. 'As the Father has loved me, I also have loved you.' The use of the aorist tense here, says Don Carson, 'probably signals the perfection, the completeness of the Father's love for his Son, including his love for him before time began.' [2] The love of the Father for the Son is so important that twice God speaks from heaven to declare it; first at the **baptism** of Jesus, his Father says to him, 'You are my beloved Son, in whom I am well pleased,' (Mark 1:11) and then, at the **transfiguration**, the Father speaks to the disciples, 'This is my beloved Son. Hear him!' (Mark 9:7). Because the Father loves the

Son—a love without beginning, a love without end and a love without limit—he has determined to bring glory to him. In one sense the whole story of redemption lies here. Though it is certainly true that God so loved the world that he gave his Son to be its Saviour, it is no less true that God so loved his Son that he gave him a people to save, a church to be his bride. In Psalm 2 the Father is represented as saying to the Son, 'Ask of me, and I will give you the nations for your inheritance, and the ends of the earth for your possession,' (verse 8). The Son asked for that costly gift, and the Father, moved by love for him, gave us to his Son.

Thirdly, it is as a reward for the work that Jesus has done. Having traced the downward steps of the Son of God, first coming as a man, a servant, then becoming obedient even to the death of the cross, Paul then comments '**Therefore** God also has highly exalted him...' At Bethlehem, the Son of God became human; at Calvary, the Son of God died as a human; now, in glory, he reigns as a human too. The human nature which the Son took in order to be born on earth has never been given up, and never will be. And as a reward for his obedience to death, the man Christ Jesus has been exalted; on the throne of heaven there reigns, for all time, a man.

Here is the key to understanding what God is doing in the world. It may not open all the locks but it certainly opens those that we are meant to open. What is God doing in the world now? He is bringing glory to Jesus. That single aim is behind the salvation of the lost—that we may acknowledge Jesus as Lord. That same aim is behind the damnation of the unbeliever—that the absolute righteousness, justice and mercy of God should be made known, and that all the world may acknowledge the uniqueness of Jesus. If God's purpose in the life of Job was simply the happiness of Job, then the book makes no sense at all. But when we read the events in heaven recorded in the first two chapters, and realise that the glory of God was at stake, then the book makes complete sense whatever questions it still leaves unanswered.

Whatever problem the unbeliever may have with these answers, we who are Christians surely ought to be able to rejoice in it. We are a people who have seen (because God has shown us) something of the glory of the Lord Jesus Christ. To us who believe he is indeed precious!

Therefore, if we have learned to love him and are learning to love him more, then anything which brings him glory should cause us to rejoice. Let me give you two illustrations of that.

When the young Spurgeon arrived in London, his ministry was such a success that the church hired the music hall at Surrey Gardens to accommodate the crowd. On October 19th 1856, some twenty thousand people had gathered to hear him when mischief makers begin to shout 'Fire'. In the panic to escape, several people were killed. Spurgeon, only 21 years old at the time, was devastated by the tragedy and for a while it was thought that he would never recover enough to preach again. He did, but could barely bring himself to speak of the sad events. He did however describe his own feelings in a thinly-veiled reference when he said, 'In the midst of calamities, whether they be the wreck of nations, the crash of empires, the heaving of revolutions, or the scourge of war, the great question which he [the Christian] asks himself, and asks of others too, is this—Is Christ's kingdom safe? In his own personal afflictions his chief anxiety is,—Will God be glorified, and will his honour be increased by it? If it be so, says he, although I be but as smoking flax, yet if the sun is not dimmed I will rejoice; and although I be a bruised reed, if the pillars of the temple are unbroken, what matters it that my reed is bruised? He finds it sufficient consolation, in the midst of all the breaking in pieces which he endures, to think that Christ's throne stands fast and firm, and that though the earth hath rocked beneath **his** feet, yet Christ standeth on a rock which can never be moved. ... It matters not what shall become of us: God hath highly exalted **him**, and given **him** a name which is above every name: that at the name of **Jesus** every knee should bow.' [3]

The second illustration is from the book of Revelation chapter 19. We are given there a glimpse of the praise of heaven, singing 'Alleluia! For the Lord God omnipotent reigns,' and it is actually the smoke of hell that first produces the praise. That is difficult for us all to grasp! But when 'the marriage of the Lamb has come, and his wife has made herself ready' (verse 7), then the only possible response for those who love him is 'Let us be glad and give him glory.'

Many questions may remain; but for the Christian who trusts God, and knows that God **is** good and that he **is** really in control in the world he has made, there can be real confidence in the face of adversity. Christians can sing, 'Whate'er my God ordains is right' and they can cry with Job 'Though he slay me, yet will I trust him.' In the midst of personal tragedy they believe, with Spafford, 'It is well, it is well, with my soul.'

When peace, like a river, attendeth my way,
When sorrows, like sea billows roll,
Whatever my lot, Thou hast taught me to say,
It is well, it is well, with my soul.

Though Satan should buffet, though trials should come,
Let this blest assurance control,
That Christ has regarded my helpless estate,
And has shed his own blood for my soul.

My sin—O the bliss of this glorious thought! -
My sin, not in part, but the whole,
Is nailed to his cross, and I bear it no more:
Praise the Lord, praise the Lord, O my soul!

For me, be it Christ, be it Christ hence to live!
If Jordan above me shall roll,
No pang shall be mine, for in death as in life
Thou wilt whisper Thy peace to my soul.

But, Lord, 'tis for Thee, for Thy coming, we wait;
The sky, not the grave, is our goal;
O trump of the angel! O voice of the Lord!
Blessèd hope! Blessèd rest of my soul.

Horatio Gates Spafford, 1828—88

Chapter 11

Chapter Notes 11

1   **Brian Edwards**, *Not by Chance.* Evangelical Press.
2   **D.A. Carson,** *The gospel according to John.* IVP.
3   **C.H. Spurgeon,** *New Park Street Pulpit,* volume 2. Pilgrim.

The rights of God

Please read Job chapters 38-42

The American Declaration of Independence is a noble document which begins with the twin ideas that all men are created equal and that all men have the right to life, liberty and the pursuit of happiness. These truths, it says, are 'self-evident'. Leaving aside the problem that it is hard to see in what sense all men are created equal (in intelligence? In wealth? In opportunity? No; certainly none of these things) it is only half a step from believing that all men have the right to **pursue** happiness to believing that 'everybody has the right to be happy.' And that idea has caused immeasurable unhappiness! 'Don't I have the right to be happy?' asks the young man when he walks out on a marriage that has become more difficult than pleasurable. 'Don't I have the right to be happy?' asks the woman who decides to abort an inconvenient baby. So men and women pursue their own rights confident in the belief that they are justified in doing so and that it is **right** to do so whatever the consequences may be for the life, liberty and happiness of others. Personal rights are considered sacred; even the concept cannot be challenged. Individuals insist on their rights and courts uphold them. But the only individual in the whole universe, it seems, who has no rights is God. Those who accept his existence regard him as a celestial slot-machine for the dispensing of aid in times of need. He is another one to whom we may appeal for our rights, but we certainly owe him no duty. When things go well with us we will ignore him; when things go badly we will rail against him: how dare he ignore our right to happiness? Who does he think he is?

It is with that kind of thinking that many people approach these last chapters of Job. As we have read the story, we have been puzzled. We were puzzled first by the dreadful losses that Job endured—his cattle, his family, his health. We were puzzled then that when the friends tried to explain what was going on, Job so often managed to show that they were wrong. Elihu has only added to our puzzlement: what is going on here? Why is Job suffering like this? We know (though he does not) about the conference in heaven; but that has not answered our questions. **Why** did God respond to Satan's taunts like that? Why has Job been allowed to suffer so much?

The beginning of chapter 38 seems to promise us an answer: 'The Lord answered Job out of the whirlwind.' At last! **Now** we are going to get some answers, now at last the mysterious providence of God will be explained!

Unanswered questions

But if that is what we think when we begin to read these chapters, we are soon disappointed. God says many things to Job in these five chapters but the one thing he does not do is explain himself. There is not even a hint here of God trying to justify his actions.

Some try to take refuge in the fact that, at the end of the story, Job has more than he had to begin with. That is undoubtedly true; his wealth was restored, his cattle were restored, he had more children. The story therefore ends happily. Job's problems were only temporary so, in the long run, we can simply ignore them, surely? We **could** if all Job had lost was his wealth and his health, or if this were not presented to us as a true story. But it is presented to us as a true story, and Job lost more than his health and wealth. So did others: there were many people who lost their lives. Those early chapters recorded the deaths of Job's servants and the deaths of his children, too. The provision of more servants for Job does not resurrect the dead! And new children may be a balm and a comfort, but they cannot make up for the loss of those who have died, as any bereaved parent will tell us.

So for us—and much more for Job, surely—all the questions are still there. Why does God allow suffering at all? Why has God allowed Job to suffer? Yet strangely, when God comes to suffering Job and begins to speak to him, it is not words of comfort, but of rebuke. And even more strangely, when Job has heard God, his reaction is to accept that rebuke, and stop complaining: 'I abhor myself, and repent in dust and ashes' (42:6). Plainly, something has happened to Job, and particularly to his understanding of God: 'I have heard of you by the hearing of the ear, but now my eye sees you, **therefore** I abhor myself...' What has God said to him that has brought about such a change?

1. The greatness of God

First, God speaks to Job about his own greatness, and forces Job to confront his ignorance and littleness. 'Who is this who darkens counsel by words without knowledge?' God asks. For almost three chapters, God challenges Job with example after example of his power, rebuking Job for daring to challenge a Creator of such awesome majesty. Job is challenged about creation: 'Prepare yourself like a man; I will question you and you shall answer me. Where were you when I laid the foundations of the earth?' (38:4). Then he is challenged about the coming of each day: is it you, Job, who commands the morning to come? (38:12). No, of course not; it is God who controls light and darkness. Does Job control the weather? 'Have you entered the treasury of snow, or have you seen the treasury of hail?' (38:22). Or the path of the thunderbolt? (38:25). Does Job control the stars, so that the constellations of Pleiades and Orion move at his command? (38:31). The answer to all of these questions of course is a resounding 'No!'; Job controls none of these things, but God controls them all. Why then has Job dared to challenge God?

God then goes on to speak of his care for the beasts of the earth: the lion, the wild goat and the deer. In all this, God is saying to Job, 'You criticise the way I govern the universe; but the truth is, you could not govern the universe **at all!**'

There is a good picture of the powerlessness of Job painted for us in the contrast between an ostrich and a stork in 39:13. 'The wings of the ostrich wave proudly,'—but Job, they are like your words—useless! The ostrich will never fly. Job has uttered unbridled words, but they accomplish nothing. **God's** words however are like those of the stork, for the stork's wings are not useless. Job has uttered words of complaint, but God's words created the universe. 'God said, 'Let there be light,' and there was light' (Genesis 1:3). Job's words are no more than an empty vapour; God's words have creating power. And all of the things God has made—the stork and the ostrich, the snow and the sea, the earth itself—all speak of his greatness and power. All of them should have given Job cause for humility. There is enough in creation around you, Job, to know that you should not answer back to God! 'For since the creation of the world [God's] invisible attributes are clearly seen, being understood by the things that are made, even his eternal power and Godhead' (Romans 1:20).

2. The justice of God

Related to the greatness of God is the justice of God. 'Would you annul my judgement?' (Or, as the NIV helpfully puts it, 'Would you discredit my justice?') 'Would you condemn me that you may be justified?' (40:8). That is what Job has been doing. Rather than admit that there are mysteries at work which he cannot understand, Job has implied that God is unrighteous; God now reminds Job that he governs the world with righteousness, humbling the proud, bringing them low and treading down the wicked (40:11,12). These are not the marks of an unjust God; would Job manage the world better?

3. The rights of God

Then, God speaks of his own rights. 'Who has preceded me that I should pay him? Everything under heaven is mine' (41:11). Here, God declares that no-one has a claim on God; he owns everything and he has absolute rights over his creation.

This is the central issue. We may assume that God owes us something; after all, he created us! It is his fault we are here, and he therefore has a duty to look after us. But God says no. That is not the case; he owes no-one anything. Even if there was an obligation of the Creator to the created, we have forfeited any claim to it. Our mutiny against the Holy God has left us completely without rights. God does not owe you, or me, anything at all.

What I have just said is perhaps the most difficult thing of all for us to accept; it goes so completely against our nature, cuts right across our pride and runs counter to every way we have ever been taught to think about ourselves. Yet it is clear; in the Bible, God has rights, man has duties. It is never the other way around. Throughout these chapters, when God at last appears to Job as he had asked, there is no hint of God beginning to explain himself or justify himself. He takes it for granted, and Job eventually agrees, that he had the right to treat Job as he wished.

But what if God behaved wickedly? Does he have the right to do that? It is an important question, but it comes from a misunderstanding of God's nature. We are used to dealing with finite, sinful human beings. If we gave absolute rights to any human it would be a recipe for disaster! We would naturally assume that, at some point, that person would behave in an evil way. But God is not a man, that he should sin; when Isaiah tells us that the angels before the throne cry, 'Holy, Holy, Holy...' he is telling us that the very nature of God is pure. He cannot sin. God **cannot** behave wickedly, so we need never fear that God will use his absolute rights in a wicked way. 'He is the Rock, his work is perfect; for all his ways are justice, a God of truth and without injustice; righteous and upright is he' (Deuteronomy 32:4). But we must be clear in our own minds that God does have rights; as the great heathen king Nebuchadnezzar was brought to confess, 'He does according to his will in the army of heaven and among the inhabitants of the earth. No one can restrain his hand or say to him, 'What have you done?'' (Daniel 4:35).

It is this question of the **rights** of God that seems to be the crucial difference between the two different theologies which are called Calvinism and Arminianism. The question that divides them is this: does God have the right to deal with different people in different ways? Or are there constraints on God that mean he has to deal with everybody in exactly the same way? In particular, the question focuses around the matter of salvation. Does God have the right to deal with people differently in the matter of their salvation? Does he have the right to choose some to salvation and yet pass over others, when 'passing over' them leaves them inevitably condemned to hell? The difference between these two understandings of salvation is not really about the sovereign **power** of God; both sides acknowledge that. The crucial difference is about the **rights** of God; does God have the right to deal with us differently? The Arminian answers, 'No; he does not have that right.' As a result, every reference in the Bible to, for example, the doctrine of election has to be interpreted in a way that denies the obvious, surface meaning. But the Calvinist answers our question quite differently. He says, 'Yes; if that is what God chooses to do, he has the right to do it. He owes nobody anything. Let God be God.' Who is right? To find an answer, we need to go into the book of Romans.

Read carefully Romans 9:20,21. 'Will the thing formed say to him who formed it, 'Why have you made me like this?' Does not the potter have power over the clay, from the same lump to make one vessel for honour and another for dishonour?' It is possible to ask a question in a way that guarantees getting the answer you want, and that is just what Paul has done here. Of course, the only answer that we can give to his question is, 'Yes, he does.' Then 'What if God, wanting to show his wrath and to make his power known, endured with much long-suffering the vessels of wrath prepared for destruction, and that he might make known the riches of his glory on the vessels of mercy which he had prepared beforehand for glory...' (Romans 9:22,23). Paul is answering our question: 'Does God have the right to deal differently with people in this matter of salvation?' and he is answering, 'Yes; God does have that right.' It is breathtaking, but it is clear what he is saying. Some people try to avoid the impact of this by saying, 'God has that right; but he never uses it. This is purely hypothetical.' But that will simply not do as a way of dealing with the problem. Let us go back a few verses to see why.

In verse 17 Paul deals with a particular case, that of Pharaoh from the time of Moses. Paul quotes from the book of Exodus: 'I have raised you up that I might show my power in you and that my name might be declared in all the earth.' How was God's name declared because of Pharaoh? God's **power** was made known as he defeated the armies of Egypt and his **love** for Israel was made known as God delivered them from Pharaoh's grasp. But for God's love and power to be made known in this way, Pharaoh's heart had to be hard, and Paul comments, '[God] has mercy on whom he wills, and whom he wills he hardens.' This is not a theoretical right; it is a right that God exercises.

If we have a problem with this it is because we cannot accept that we have no claim on God. But according to the Bible, when God gives good things, it is grace; grace is receiving good things that we do not deserve. A story from the time of Napoleon makes this point well. A young soldier in Napoleon's army had committed an offence and been sentenced to death, and his mother gained an audience with the

Emperor himself to plead for her son's life. 'Lord,' she said, 'Have mercy on my son.' Napoleon sent for the details of the case and, when he had heard them, answered, 'Woman, your son does not deserve mercy.' 'No, Lord,' she replied; 'If he deserved it, it would not **be** mercy. Have **mercy** on my son.' I do not know whether her plea was successful or not, but I do know that she had understood grace and mercy! If we deserve it, it cannot be grace. If we do not deserve God's grace, then he does not have to give it to us. He can choose to withhold it from us all, or he can choose to withhold it from nobody. **Or** he can choose to withhold it from some but not from others. That is his right. We must face this reality; we deserve nothing from God but our condemnation. To ask for fairness from God is to ask for hell.

This teaching is often misrepresented. It is sometimes expressed as if all mankind were gathered together on the edge of a cliff, quite safe, until God came along and pushed some over that cliff to the rocks of damnation below. But Don Carson is right when he says, 'We must always remember that the Bible does not present us with a God who chances upon neutral men and women and arbitrarily consigns some to heaven and some to hell. He takes guilty men and women, all of whom deserve his wrath, and in his great mercy and love he saves vast numbers of them. Had he saved only one, it would have been an act of grace; that he saves a vast host affirms still more unmistakably the uncharted reaches of that grace. From a biblical perspective, hell stands as a horrible witness to human defiance in the face of great grace.' [1] Man has jumped off the cliff himself; and he has done so in spite of the fact that God has (as it were) put up abundant notices on the edge saying, 'Danger; Do Not Approach!'

But **why** has he chosen to save some and not others? Given that he has the right to do so, is there anything we can say from the Scriptures about why he has exercised that right? Paul answers this question with a question of his own: 'What if God, wanting to show his wrath and to make his power known, endured with much long-suffering the vessels of wrath prepared for destruction, ... that he might make known the riches of his glory on the vessels of mercy, which he had prepared beforehand for glory' (Romans 9:22,23). Paul is saying clearly that in order that we who are saved might appreciate the glory and wonder of his salvation clearly, God has allowed some not to experience it. His point is easy to understand: for how could we have **really** known how abundant, how amazing, God's grace is if we had never seen the alternative? It is not understanding Paul that people find difficult; it is accepting the truth of what he says.

One objection to this truth that often comes up is this: 'If God is really sovereign over everything, if nothing happens which is outside his will, then why does he blame us for our sin?' It is this very objection that Paul has dealt with a few verses earlier: 'Why does he still find fault? For who has resisted his will?' The answer Paul gives brings us back to Job: 'Indeed, O man, who are you to reply against God?' (verse 20). When he deals with what is surely **the** ultimate question, Paul has to admit that there are mysteries; but those mysteries should not make us challenge God. We have to remember who we are talking to; we have to remember that he is God and we are mortals, and sinful, fallen mortals at that.

God has rights; and if that is so in the matter of our salvation, it is true too in the matter of human suffering. We must not be arrogant and talk back to God: 'Do not be rash with your mouth, and let not your heart utter anything hastily before God. For God is in heaven, and you on earth; therefore let your words be few' (Ecclesiastes 5:2).

What then does this say to us? We must not so justify ourselves, either as individuals or as mankind, in a way that makes God guilty. When we are going through trials we are not entitled to say that God is being unfair to us. Nor are we entitled to look at the scheme of God's salvation and his glorious, glorious mercy, and say that it is not fair; for grace is not fair! We must recognise instead that we have no claim on God, and that his grace is gloriously free. In order to save us from the rocks of damnation God did not merely reach out an arm to save us; rather (to keep to the picture, imperfect though it is) he threw himself on the rocks that he might cushion our fall with his own body. In order to save us it took the death of his Son. This is the greatest mystery of them all: the mystery of his grace, that he was willing to save us at such a cost.

For we who are Christians know more about the God we trust than Job did. When he could only cry in the darkness, 'though he slay me yet will I trust him...' (13:15), we can say in the light, 'God demonstrates his own love toward us, in that while we were still sinners, Christ died for us' (Romans 5:8). In the cross we see two vital things: the greatness of the love of God, and the certainty of his grace towards us. However much suffering may come to us, we can take refuge in the fact that Jesus too, our God, has suffered. He suffered 'unfairly' (for the Lord Jesus did not deserve the cross) and he suffered for us. When he cried out 'My God, my God, why have you forsaken me?' he suffered more and descended lower than Job had, and lower than we will. If he suffered that for us, we may be sure that his purpose towards us is ultimately good. We may believe that our sufferings work for our good, and that he will bring us through them to glory. 'He who did not spare his own Son, but delivered him up for us all, how shall he not with him also freely give us all things?' (Romans 8:32).

Job's sufferings ...

Job has suffered; now his sufferings are passed. But still he has no answer: why has God allowed this? He still knows nothing of the events in heaven recorded in the first two chapters. He still does not know that God has staked his own reputation on Job's integrity. But God has been vindicated, and that is important. The unbeliever will never accept God's failure to answer Job's questions, or ours; but that is because the unbeliever will never be content not to be God. But those who do know God will learn much from knowing what answers are **not** true. They will learn from Job to look beyond this life, not for answers (which may not come even in heaven) but for the Redeemer, who has conquered death for us and will raise us to be with him. They will remember 'that the sufferings of this present time are not worthy to be compared with the glory which shall be revealed in us,' (Romans 8:18). Then, hopefully, they will learn that it is better to know God, and trust God, than to demand answers.

...trusting God...

For Job does trust God; he emerges from his trials having demonstrated that he serves God out of a pure heart. He has learned along the way; he has learned about himself, and he has learned to stop accusing God of a lack of justice. He has demonstrated too the truth of something that an apostle would articulate centuries later: 'God is faithful, who will not allow you to be tempted beyond what you are able' (1 Corinthians 10:13). Job has indeed been tempted to the limit, but not beyond it. In this, God can be trusted.

...and things too wonderful

When Job sees God, he confesses 'I have uttered what I did not understand, things too wonderful for me which I did not know' (42:3). These words should be in the introduction to every book of systematic theology: 'things too wonderful for me.' For when Job sees God, and hears what God has to say, he repents: 'Therefore I abhor myself and repent in dust and ashes.' He has no complaints left—except about himself!

So it will be eventually with us: whether it is in the matter of our own suffering or in the matter of God's sovereign dealing with the children of men, when judgement day comes every mouth will be stopped (Romans 3:19). Nobody will have a word of rebuke to bring against God when they see him. Every mouth will be stopped—until the mouths of the redeemed are opened again to sing: 'Hallelujah, for the Lord God omnipotent reigns.'

Chapter 12. Note

1   **D.A. Carson,** *How long, O Lord?* IVP.

Genesis for today

Andy McIntosh

Large format paperback
208 pages   £6.99

"You can't be a scientist and take the book of Genesis as literal history!"
Andy McIntosh is a scientist, and is one who also believes that the book of Genesis is literal history and is foundational to the rest of Scripture. In no way does Genesis conflict with the real science he is conducting at Leeds University. The author, though, has come to understand something that the church in the United Kingdom has lost—that ultimately all Christian doctrine, directly or indirectly, is founded in the literal events of the first eleven chapters of the Bible. He believes that the foundation of Christianity has been undermined and all but destroyed in England because much of the church has accepted the fallible theories of evolution; all Christian doctrines are dependent on the literal events of Genesis.
This book will play an active role in a growing world-wide movement to bring reformation again to a church which has sadly compromised the clear teaching of Scripture, particularly regarding the foundational book of Genesis.

Reference: Gen
ISBN 0 902548 78 6

The Lord's Prayer for today

Derek Prime

Large format paperback
163 pages   £5.95

The Lord's Prayer is the only pattern prayer the Lord Jesus provided and is timeless in purpose and function. It indicates how we are to pray throughout our life in this present world. Its truths do not change. It is essential for us us to be reminded of them. The Lord's Prayer reminds us, at its very beginning, that true worship of God arises from a living relationship with Him as our Father through our Lord Jesus Christ.

Derek Prime was for many years the pastor of Charlotte Baptist Chapel, Edinburgh. He is now a well-known convention speaker and author of many books including *Let's Say The Grace Together* and *Gofors and Grumps.*

Reference: LP
ISBN 0 902548 68 9

For further information about other Day One titles, call or write to us:

01372 728 300

In Europe: ++ 44 1372 728 300

In North America: 011 44 1372 728 300

Day One 3 Epsom Business Park Kiln Lane Epsom Surrey KT17 1JF England

e-mail address: ldos.dayone@ukonline.co.uk

Also from Day One

The Ten Commandments for today

Brian H. Edwards

Large format paperback
288 pages   **£8.99**

At a time when the nation's morality is in alarming decline, it is surprising that so little has been written on the Ten Commandments. Brian Edwards gives us a modern commentary, carefully uncovering their true meaning and incisively applying them to our contemporary society. Probably never in the history of western civilisation have the Ten Commandments been more neglected and therefore more relevant than today.

With more than 30 years in a pastoral and preaching ministry, **Brian Edwards** has authored a number of books including *God's Outlaw*, a biography of William Tyndale, and the study of Biblical authority, *Nothing but the truth*. He also wrote the popular *In Conversation* series published by Day One, and co-authored with his wife Barbara the marriage preparation course, *No Longer Two*.

ISBN 0 902548 69 7

The Beatitudes for Today

John Blanchard

Large format paperback
263 pages   **£7.95**

In his foreword, Eric J. Alexander writes, "this book fills a significant gap in contemporary Christian writing. Although the past thirty years have seen the publication of several excellent volumes on the Sermon on the Mount, we have lacked a full-length treatment of the Beatitudes. The Christian world has been deeply indebted to John Blanchard for his preaching and writing ministry over many years. Both are characterised by an absolute faithfulness to the text of Scripture, a deep concern to apply God's Word to today's world, and a God-given insight into the implications of biblical truth."

John Blanchard is an internationally known British Evangelist and Bible teacher, who has written a number of best-selling books including *Ultimate Questions, Right with God, Pop Goes the Gospel* and *Whatever Happened to Hell?*

ISBN 0 902548 67 0

For further information about other Day One titles, call or write to us:

01372 728 300

In Europe: ++ 44 1372 728 300

In North America: 011 44 1372 728 300

Day One 3 Epsom Business Park Kiln Lane Epsom Surrey KT17 1JF England

e-mail address: ldos.dayone@ukonline.co.uk